Cook Like a Peasant, Eat Like a King

Cook Like a

Peasant, Eat Like a King

by Maria Luisa Scott and
Jack Denton Scott

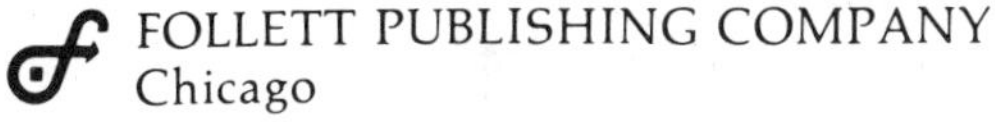
FOLLETT PUBLISHING COMPANY
Chicago

Manufactured in the United States of America.

This is for Maria Cifelli Limoncelli and Pasquale Limoncelli, who made simple foods superb. And for Antoine Gilly, who makes complicated foods simple.

Contents

Our thanks to Edward T. Thompson
for the title and for his encouragement

"Peasant cuisine is the basis of the culinary art. . . ." Alexandre Dumaine

THE JAPANESE have a way of cutting right to the heart of any situation. Not long ago a television production company in Tokyo wanted to make a short film showing how expert the French were at converting simple foods into table masterpieces. They went to three-star chef Alain Chapel for help in finding a talented farmer's wife. Without hesitation, he recommended a peasant woman in Mionnay. With two of France's top three-star chefs standing by to assist her, if needed (they didn't lift a hand), that farm woman gave a spectacular demonstration of peasant proficiency, preparing a dinner in which *everything* came from her own farm.

Paul Bocuse, one of the most talked-about chefs in France, immediately got on that bandwagon, declaring that the patron saint of all chefs should be a composite of those peasant wives whose uncomplicated cooking does such honor to France's fine foods.

We had that feeling and made that discovery long ago—in three stages. Stage one took place when this team left New York City and moved onto 138 acres in Roxbury, Connecticut—and, in effect, became peasants ourselves.

A moment here while we define *peasant*. Too often the word is used in a derogatory sense for "clod or oaf," when it really should be synonymous with dignity and decency. The best dictionary we could find lists, "Peasant. n. A member of the class comprising small farmers and laborers on the land where these constitute the main labor force in agriculture."

The Italians say it even better: *contadino,* "countryman," a person who lives in a rural area. This has to mean that peasants are smarter than anyone else. For these are the people who do not have to live in the pollution, filth, and nerve-wracking turmoil of cities, where crime and welfare have become a way of life. Country people do not commit crimes (except, rarely, of passion) and they do not know the meaning of welfare, which rapidly is becoming the wrap-up word for the twentieth century. Peasants ably take care of themselves almost from the moment they are born and are, and always have been, suspicious of something for nothing. Thus, they were onto the politicians long before the rest of us. But enough, this is not a book about philosophy, but about the food of country folk.

And that is the way we became peasants—through raising food ourselves, learning the hard law of living from the land. For two decades we raised our own vegetables, chickens, eggs, Cornish game hens, geese, rabbits, pigeons, pigs, sheep, turkeys. We fed those turkeys (raising only the more delicate hens) the corn we grew, mixed with molasses. The flavor of those birds was such that we felt we were some kind of geniuses, until we learned what it cost to bring a hen turkey to the harvesting stage.

This peasant existence was not without its amusing aspects either. One night we were in the cellar assessing our canned goods when we discovered that we had (for the two of us!) 350 quart jars of tomatoes. Another time (because of our liking for Italian sausage) we discovered, with some dismay, that we had converted three Yorkshire pigs into nothing but sweet Italian sausage! No hams, no bacon, no roasts.

Stage two in our discovery of the true value of simple food was tied in with the male member of the team's writing profession. Researching for material and simple curiosity took us around the world more than a dozen times, with long stopovers in Europe. It didn't take long for us to discover that the most interesting food wasn't found in the three-star restaurants and the culinary capitals. The dishes we enjoyed most were prepared in villages or in farm homes, and the recipes for many of them are in this book.

We also discovered that peasants are poets of the earth. A Spanish farmer who raised squashes for the market on a small plot of earth called his produce "daughters of my soul." He had names for each, and when he watered them by hand, he told us he was giving his "children" a drink.

We once had lunch and a lesson in philosophy in a market town in France with a farmer who raised grapes. He insisted that we eat a dish of white onions simmered in sweet butter and lavishly flamed with brandy. This would insure that we could drink wine from noon to dusk without a wobble. It seemed to work too, as a sort of transcendental meditation of the table–or of the glass.

In Europe we also saw peasant frugality convert a cheap cut of meat into a feast; frogs caught in swamps become princely fare; the herring, which is far from being the aristocrat of fishes, transformed by imagination into fine food; and sour cream help change cabbage, meats, and stews into minor symphonies.

Stage three in our discovery came about because of our friendship with Antoine Gilly, one of the greatest of French chefs. Born in rural Burgundy, he learned to cook at age nine at the elbow of his grandmother and went on to cook for King George V of England, the Prince of Wales, Prime Minister Lloyd George, and many other greats and near greats. He also established La Crémaillère, one of the most successful and highly honored French restaurants in the United States. Most appreciated of Antoine Gilly's offerings were his peasant dishes such as *cassoulet*. The Prince of Wales liked stews, the king of England, simply cooked leg of lamb. "The greater the man," M. Gilly says, "the simpler the food."

Antoine Gilly was also one of the first to say, "Go to the peasant, gourmet."

This brilliant and humble man taught us much. We have worked (and learned) for many hours with him in our kitchen and in his. Out of that came a book, *Feast of France,* that we wrote together. Out of that friendship and association also came large segments of this book, where we put what we learned into action.

This is not a book by two people. Here, in addition to our original recipes and family recipes, are others that we picked up in many parts of the world–from friends, chefs, farmers, fishermen, restaurant owners. Thus we owe much to many. We thank them here.

There are, of course, peasants in America, and enough material for a book of their recipes. But (with several exceptions) we have played favorites and concentrated on Europe, the places and people we know best. After all, many of us, perhaps most of us, originally came from Europe. And so did most of our knowledge of food.

M.L.S., J.D.S.

CHAPTER ONE

Appetizers

All country folk take their tasty tidbits with wine or other drinks before dinner. Probably the most famous of these delicacies is the Italian antipasto, which is a large platter of cold food—artichoke hearts, beans and tuna, cold marinated mushrooms, ripe olives, pimientos, radishes, anchovies, sardines, capocollo (smoked pork), pepperoni (spicy sausage), prosciutto (ham), salami—the offering limited only by the imagination. A farm family in Italy might follow that antipasto with chicken soup, pasta, then sausage, roast chicken, fried eggplant, a finocchio salad, probably fruit for dessert, and coffee. Wine would be generously poured all through the meal.

These special appetizers before dining relax the guests and tempt the taste buds for what is to come. The French call theirs *hors d'oeuvre variés,* the Germans *vorspeise,* the Middle Easterners *meze,* the Scandinavians *smörgåsbord,* Americans "the cocktail hour." The term for appetizers means the same in all languages, "before the meal."

Here we offer those that we have enjoyed in Europe and elsewhere. Most of them are quite simple, yet different. For example, try one of our favorites: Beans and Tuna, a specialty in the north of Italy.

BAGNA CAUDA

ITALY

Serves 8

This fun dish of raw vegetables dipped in a surprisingly tasty sauce is a classic one. Rarely have guests tried it. The variety of vegetables you can serve is endless. We list our preferences.

12 raw broccoli flowerettes
12 raw cauliflower flowerettes
12 raw, tender asparagus tips
12 whole, small red radishes
12 raw, tender young scallions
6 ribs from a celery heart, cut in strips ½ inch wide
3 small carrots, cut in strips ¼ inch wide
3 very small zucchini, cut in ½-inch strips
3 c heavy cream
4 T (½ stick) butter
9 flat anchovies, drained of oil, minced
2 medium-sized garlic cloves, minced
pinch of cayenne

Soak all of the vegetables (except the zucchini) in a large bowl of ice water in the refrigerator for 2 hours. To serve, dry them very well and arrange them attractively on a large platter. They should be very crisp and cold. The dipping sauce should be kept warm on an electric hot tray, a candle warmer, or any other similar device.

Boil the cream in a saucepan until it thickens; then reduce the heat to a simmer and stir constantly until the quantity is reduced by one-half. In another saucepan melt the butter and stir in the anchovies and the garlic, cooking until the garlic is just soft but not brown. Mash anchovies as smooth as possible. Blend in the cream and cayenne. Bring the sauce to a simmer. Remove from the heat, place over whatever warming device you have, and let the fun commence.

BEANS AND TUNA

ITALY

Serves 8

1 lb dry Great Northern beans
4 c chicken broth
5 garlic cloves
2 (each 7-oz) cans of Bumble Bee fancy solid white tuna, drained
4 T olive oil
juice of 1 large lemon
4 T minced Italian broad-leafed parsley
salt and pepper to taste

Pick over the beans, discarding the dark and imperfect ones. Soak them in cold water for five hours. Drain the beans, and place them in a large pot; cover them with the chicken broth and add the garlic. Bring to a boil, cover, lower heat, and simmer *very* slowly until beans are just tender. Two steps are important here: slow cooking so that the chicken broth barely shivers over the beans; and timing, so that the beans are cooked but still firm. When they are cooked, most of the liquid will be gone. Do not discard what is left. Remove the garlic. Cool the beans; then place them, with their liquid, in a large bowl. Add the tuna, broken into chunks slightly larger than bite size, the olive oil, lemon juice, and parsley. Season with salt and pepper and gently toss. Taste for seasoning, then refrigerate until time to serve. Serve on small plates with crusty buttered bread–not too much or your guests won't want dinner. We also find this an ideal luncheon on a hot summer day.

BROCCOLI, HAM, AND RICOTTA CROSTATA

ITALY

Serves 6

3 T butter
1 small white onion, minced
1½ c frozen, chopped broccoli, cooked according to package directions, thoroughly drained
½ c prosciutto or boiled ham, coarsely chopped
¼ t mace
salt and pepper to taste
2 whole eggs
2 egg yolks
1½ c medium cream
1 c ricotta (thoroughly drained in a strainer)
¾ c grated Parmesan cheese
1 10-inch partially baked pastry shell

Heat the butter in a saucepan and sauté the onion until it is soft and transparent. Remove from the heat and stir in the broccoli, ham, mace, salt, and pepper. In a bowl beat together the eggs, egg yolks, cream, ricotta, and half of the Parmesan cheese. Combine the broccoli-ham mixture with the egg-cream-ricotta mixture. Spoon the mixture into the pastry shell. Sprinkle the remaining Parmesan on top, place the *crostata* on a baking sheet, and bake in a preheated 375-degree oven for 30 minutes or until set (a knife blade inserted halfway between crust and center comes out clean), puffed, and golden on top. If the top browns before the *crostata* is set, cover loosely with a sheet of aluminum foil. Do not overcook. Serve immediately.

HUNGARIAN COTTAGE CHEESE MIX

Serves 6

6 T butter, softened, not melted
½ lb large curd cottage cheese, pushed through a sieve
1 T paprika (Hungarian is best)
1 t crushed caraway seeds
1 small white onion, finely minced
1½ t capers, drained, minced
½ c sour cream
salt and pepper to taste
1½ T minced parsley
1½ T minced chives

In a mixing bowl cream the butter by rapidly beating it against the side of the bowl with a wooden spoon. Blend in cottage cheese, paprika, caraway seeds, onion, capers, and sour cream. Season with salt and pepper. The Hungarians use a strong right arm and the wooden spoon to beat this into a smooth paste spread. You can use an electric mixer. Refrigerate it until it just begins to set; then shape it into any form you like. Roll it in the parsley and chives and refrigerate for 3 hours. It can be sliced or used as a spread with drinks.

CHEESE STRAWS

ENGLAND

Serves 8

2 c flour
½ t salt
½ lb very sharp Cheddar cheese at room temperature
½ lb (2 sticks) firm butter
flour for rolling out pastry
1 egg, beaten
3 T salt
2 heaping T poppy seeds

Sift the flour and salt together. Chop cheese finely, or put through the medium blade of a grinder. In a bowl thoroughly mix the flour, cheese, and butter, using a pastry cutter; then, with your hands, form the dough into 2 balls. Wrap the balls in plastic wrap and refrigerate them until they are firm enough to handle. Sprinkle the top and bottom of the balls with flour and between two sheets of wax paper roll each into a ¼-inch-thick sheet. With a pastry cutter, cut the sheets into strips of any width you desire. Classically they are cut narrow so that when baked, they are slightly larger than straws. When cut, lay the strips on a cookie sheet, paint them lightly with the beaten egg. Lightly sprinkle them with salt and poppy seeds. Place in a preheated 350-degree oven for 15 minutes or until the cheese straws are golden.

CHICKEN TERRINE

FRANCE

Serves 10

This dish is named for the container in which it is cooked. *Terrine,* from *terra,* means "an earthenware dish." It can be square, oblong, or oval and is deep. What it traditionally contains is delightful and among our favorite foods. The words *pâtés* and *terrines* are often used interchangeably, but our notion is that a *pâté* is more finely textured and creamier, while the *terrine* is somewhat coarser and lustier. Either can be crowned with a crust, but country folk leave that to the fancy restaurants. They put their favorite recipe to bake in an earthenware dish and place it on the sideboard, where guests can cut a slice at will. A *terrine* on the sideboard is also a sure sign that you are in the hands of a host, or hostess, who takes cooking seriously, as all of us peasants do. We like *terrines* with toast as an appetizer, for a summer lunch, or as a first course at dinner. This is a simple one, made in France during the wine harvest, with rabbit as the main ingredient. Although we also prefer rabbit, we have substituted chicken so that the squeamish won't miss this taste treat.

If you haven't a *terrine,* a loaf-shaped Pyrex baking dish, large enough so that the ingredients will come slightly higher than the sides of the baking dish, will work very well.

2½ lb chicken breasts and thighs (after boning)
1 lb Tobin's First Prize Pork for Beans (fatback with streaks of lean meat)
¾ lb uncooked ham
1 lb white onions, chopped
3 cloves garlic, minced
1 t dry thyme
1½ t salt
1 t black pepper
1 c dry white wine
¼ c brandy
3 T flour
3 small eggs
18 slices bacon, blanched, dried

Put the chicken, fat, and ham through the coarse blade of your grinder. In a bowl, with your hands, mix the onions, garlic, thyme, salt, pepper, wine, and brandy with the ground meats. Marinate in the refrigerator for 5 hours. At the end of that time, take a couple of spoonfuls of liquid from the bowl in which the ground meats marinated and blend into the flour to make a mixture the thickness of cream. Beat the eggs into this and blend well with the ground meat mixture.

Line the bottom and sides of the *terrine* with the bacon strips so they lap over the sides. (After you fill the *terrine* with the chicken mixture, you can bring the lapped portion of the bacon strips over to cover it. The chicken mixture will then be encased in bacon strips.) Spoon the meat into the *terrine*. When filled, lap the bacon over it, as explained, and cover with foil and a lid. Place the *terrine* in a pan that has about an inch of hot water in it. Bake in a preheated 300-degree oven for 3½ hours. Remove and cool for another 4 hours, without removing the cover or the foil. Discard the bacon. This *terrine* will keep well in the refrigerator for a week.

CHICKEN LIVERS

GERMANY

Serves 6

- **4 T of rendered pork fat**
- **1 lb chicken livers, cleaned, washed, dried**
- **2 small white onions, chopped**
- **2 medium-sized, hard-boiled eggs**
- **salt and pepper to taste**

Heat 2 tablespoons pork fat in a frying pan and sauté the chicken livers 7 minutes. Remove the livers. In the same pan sauté the onions in the remaining pork fat until soft and transparent. Chop the livers, the eggs, and the onions together. Put through the fine blade of a food grinder. Place in a bowl, season to taste with salt and pepper, and blend in the pork fat left in the frying pan. Place the chopped livers in a serving bowl, pack down, and chill for 2 hours. The Germans serve this cold with thin black bread.

TUSCAN CHICKEN LIVERS ON TOAST

ITALY

Serves 6

4 oz (1 stick) butter
4 T finely chopped onion
8 chicken livers, cleaned, washed, dried
salt and pepper to taste
pinch of marjoram
pinch of oregano
3 T Marsala wine
2 T chopped parsley
a narrow (about 2½ to 3 inches in diameter) loaf of Italian or French bread

In a frying pan sauté the onions in the butter until they are soft. Add the chicken livers, sprinkle with salt, pepper, marjoram, and oregano and sauté them until they start to brown. Add the Marsala, raising the heat to cook off the moisture. While the livers are still pink and juicy inside, transfer them to a chopping board; then continue to cook down the liquid in the frying pan. Finely chop the livers. Transfer them with the contents of the frying pan and the parsley to a bowl and mash them all together. Cut 18 thin slices from the loaf of bread. Toast them on one side, butter the untoasted sides with soft butter, mound the mixture on top, and put under a broiler just long enough to heat them a little.

MIDDLE EASTERN CUCUMBERS

Serves 8

2 small cucumbers
4 young scallions (white part only), minced
½ t each, salt and black pepper
¼ t cumin powder
⅛ t curry powder
½ c natural yogurt
thin rounds of buttered bread the size of cucumber slices

Peel the cucumbers and cut them into thin slices. Place on a paper towel. Cover with another towel with a heavy weight atop for 15 minutes to press out excess moisture. In a bowl combine the scallions, salt, pepper, cumin, curry powder, and the yogurt, blending well. Refrigerate cucumbers and yogurt mixture. Spoon some of the yogurt atop each cucumber slice and serve very cold on the bread.

SICILIAN EGGPLANT

Serves 8

2 medium-sized eggplants
1 c olive oil
5 small white onions, sliced
1 c (8 oz) tomato sauce
3 ribs celery, scraped and diced
½ c dry white wine
2 T capers, drained
10 black olives, pitted, sliced
2 T pignoli (pine nuts)
½ c wine vinegar
3 T sugar
salt and pepper to taste

Peel the eggplants and cut them into 1-inch cubes. In a large saucepan sauté the cubes in ¾ cup of the olive oil, browning them evenly. Remove with a slotted spoon and drain on paper towel. If all of the oil has been absorbed by the eggplant, pour the remaining oil into the saucepan and sauté the onions until they are golden. Pour off the oil and add the tomato sauce and celery. Simmer until celery is tender, midway stirring in the wine. Stir in the capers, olives, pignoli, and the browned eggplant. In another saucepan heat the vinegar, stir in the sugar, and simmer until the sugar has dissolved. Pour over the eggplant and season with salt and pepper. Simmer, uncovered, stirring often but carefully, for 15 minutes. Refrigerate for 4 hours. Traditionally this *caponatina* appetizer is served cold with crusty bread.

GUACAMOLE

MEXICO

Serves 6

2 medium-sized, ripe avocados, mashed
1 T finely minced onion
2 T fresh lemon juice
2 T chili sauce mixed with 4 drops Tabasco sauce (Mexicans use tomatoes and very hot chilis, but we find this an excellent substitute)
1 t fresh coriander (cilantro) or parsley, minced
salt and pepper to taste
1 large garlic clove, mashed
Fritos or tortilla chips for dipping
1 small, white head of cauliflower, raw, divided into flowerettes for dipping in the guacamole

In a large bowl combine the mashed avocados, onion, lemon juice, chili sauce with Tabasco sauce, coriander or parsley, salt, and pepper. Blend well. Rub a serving bowl well with the mashed garlic, and discard the garlic. Fill the bowl with the guacamole and place it in the center of a serving tray, surrounding it with the corn chips and cauliflower.

HERRING IN WHIPPED CREAM

SCANDINAVIA

Serves 6

Different versions of this dish are served in Norway, Sweden, Denmark, and Finland. The Danes are fond of this one. They use salt herring, but herring in jars works very well.

2 (each 5 oz) jars Bismarck herring, cut into ½-inch cubes
4 small potatoes, boiled, cooled, and cut into ½-inch cubes
6 small beets, boiled, cooled, and cut into ½-inch cubes
2 small white onions, thinly sliced
2 T wine vinegar
2 t Dijon-type mustard
2 t sugar
salt and pepper to taste
1 c whipping cream, whipped

In a large bowl combine the herring, potatoes, beets, onions, vinegar, mustard, sugar. Season with salt and pepper and mix well. Chill. Stir in the whipped cream just before serving.

LAMB TIDBITS

GREECE

Serves 6

2 lb lean lamb from the leg, cut into small cubes
salt and pepper
juice of 3 lemons mixed with 2 t dry oregano

Skewer the cubes of lamb, dividing them into 6 equal portions. Sprinkle all over with salt and pepper. Cook over charcoal (or under a broiler), turning frequently so the meat browns evenly. Do not overcook; the lamb should be pink and juicy inside. Eight minutes should do it, but time depends on the size of the cubes. Pour the lemon juice-oregano mixture into a wide flat plate. Roll the lamb on the skewers in this mixture and broil for 20 seconds on each side.

MOZZARELLA CHEESE IN A CARRIAGE

ITALY

Serves 6

These fried mozzarella sandwiches, found all over Italy in great variety, are traditionally made from 3-inch rounds of bread. We are cutting the rounds smaller for easy finger-eating with cocktails.

24 bread rounds (no crusts), cut ¼ inch thick, 2 inches in diameter from firm bread such as Italian or French
12 ¼-inch-thick slices of mozzarella cheese, cut in the same shape as the bread but slightly smaller
about ½ c milk
about 1 c fine bread crumbs
3 eggs beaten with 2 T milk
fat or oil for frying

Make 12 sandwiches of the bread and mozzarella. Dip the edges of the sandwiches in the milk, press them together to seal in the cheese, and then dip them in bread crumbs. Now dip the whole sandwich in the egg-and-milk mixture, then into the bread crumbs, paying special attention to covering the edges. Fry the sandwiches in ½ inch of preheated fat or oil (365 to 375 degrees) until golden. Drain on paper towels and serve hot.

Mozzarella cheese can be prepared without the bread. Cut the cheese into any size piece you like (cubes or oblongs) depending upon whether you want them to be eaten with the fingers or served on a plate and eaten with a fork. If you prefer the latter, cut into a larger size.

Dredge the pieces of cheese with flour and shake off any excess. Dip them in the beaten egg and milk, then in the fine bread crumbs, and then back into the egg and the bread crumbs again; then fry them in the fat. Cheese will maintain shape better if fried while cold.

ASIAN MUSHROOMS

Serves 8

½ c soy sauce
¼ c vinegar
2 T sugar
3 garlic cloves, minced
1½ lb small mushrooms, stems removed, cleaned

Combine soy sauce, vinegar, sugar, and garlic in a saucepan and simmer, uncovered, for 2 minutes; cool to warm. Place the mushrooms in a bowl, pour in the warm marinade, and refrigerate at least 4 hours, stirring from time to time. Drain and serve cold.

JAPANESE MUSSELS AND SHRIMPS

Serves 8

1 c sake (rice wine) or light sherry
2 T sugar
32 mussels, shells removed
32 small shrimp (about 1¼ lb), shelled and deveined
½ c soy sauce

Bring the sake (or sherry) and sugar to a simmer in a saucepan, stirring until the sugar has dissolved. Add the mussels and simmer, uncovered, for 1 minute. Stir in the shrimp and simmer for 2 minutes. Pour in the soy sauce and simmer for another minute. With a slotted spoon remove the mussels and shrimp. Boil the liquid in the pan until it has thickened enough to coat a spoon. Remove from the fire and return the mussels and shrimp to the pan, blending them with the sauce until they are thoroughly coated. Chill and serve.

NIÇOISE TART

FRANCE

Serves 6

4 medium-sized, yellow onions (about 1 lb), chopped
3 T butter
1 T olive oil
salt and pepper to taste
4 medium-sized, ripe tomatoes, skin removed, seeded, and coarsely chopped
6 flat anchovy fillets
12 black olives, pitted
1 9-inch pastry shell, partially baked

Sauté the onions in the butter and oil for 20 minutes or until they are soft but not brown. Season with salt and pepper. In a saucepan simmer the tomatoes for 15 minutes or until most of the liquid has cooked off. Season them with salt and pepper. Line the bottom of the pastry shell with the onions. Spoon the cooked tomatoes over the onions. Arrange the anchovies like spokes in a wheel on top of the tomatoes and arrange the olives on the tomatoes between the "spokes." Place on a baking sheet and bake in a preheated 400-degree oven for 35 minutes or until the edge of the pastry is golden.

ONION QUICHE

FRANCE

Serves 6

6 medium-sized, yellow onions, sliced
3 T butter
1 T olive oil
salt and pepper to taste
6 strips bacon, cooked until crisp, drained, and diced
1 partially baked 9-inch pastry shell
3 eggs
1 egg yolk
1½ c medium cream
¾ c grated Gruyère cheese
pinch of nutmeg
few grains of cayenne

Sauté the onions in 2 tablespoons of butter and the oil until they are soft but not brown. Season with salt and pepper. Sprinkle the bacon over the bottom of the pastry shell. Then distribute the onions over the bacon. Beat the eggs, egg yolk, cream, ½ cup of the cheese, nutmeg, cayenne, and a sprinkle of salt and pepper in a bowl until well mixed; then carefully pour over the onions. Sprinkle the remaining cheese on top and dot with the remaining tablespoon of butter. Set on a baking sheet and bake in a preheated 375-degree oven for 30 minutes or until set (a knife blade inserted halfway between crust and center will come out clean), puffed, and golden on top. If the top browns before the custard sets, cover lightly with a sheet of aluminum foil.

SAUSAGE IN A CRUST

Serves 6

This is popular in several European countries, and although farm families there often use it as an appetizer or for a luncheon, restaurants here and abroad have elevated it to a very special first course for dinner that has won renown for some of them. The trick is in making the crust, but it is well worth the effort. If you want to serve this to guests with drinks before dinner, make the dough that morning. It is a special *brioche* dough and has its own technique. Any of a number of garlic boiling sausages can be used. We like the Italian *cotechino*.

Brioche Dough

½ package yeast (active dry)	**½ t salt**
¼ c lukewarm milk	**2 eggs**
1½ c flour	**8 T (1 stick) butter, softened**
1 t sugar	**1 14-oz cotechino sausage**

In a small bowl mix the yeast and milk, forming a paste. Set aside. In a large bowl place the flour, sugar, and salt. Make a well in the center of the flour and break the eggs into it. Add the yeast paste. Fold the flour over the eggs and yeast paste and knead into a smooth mixture. With your hands work the softened butter into this. Knead this dough well again into a firm ball. In another bowl sprinkle a little flour; place the ball of dough on it. With a knife make a deep slash across the ball of dough. Cover it with a clean towel; then put it in a warm area for 2 hours. (Our stove has a warmer, which is ideal. Your oven turned to its lowest temperature for a few moments and then turned off can also be used.) In this length of time the ball of dough should have doubled in volume. Break this up and knead it again into a ball. Cover it and put it in a cool place until about an hour before baking.

The Sausage

Place the sausage in a pot and cover with cold water. Bring water just to a boil, lower the heat, and simmer for 1 hour. Remove and cool the sausage enough so that you can take off the skin. Keep the sausage warm.

The Crust

Rub a baking sheet lightly with butter. Place the dough in the center, lightly sprinkle it with flour, and with your hands spread or pull the dough (which should be very malleable by now) into a flat rectangular shape. Turn it completely over onto the baking sheet so the floured side is down. Place the warm sausage in the center. Fold and roll the dough around the sausage so that it is completely encased and has the shape of a very large sausage. Dip your hands into cold water and pinch the seam edges together along the top and the ends. Dip a pastry brush (or use your fingers) into cream and paint the entire upper surface and the exposed sides. This will glaze the roll. With a knife, make light criss-cross marks in the center. Let the roll stand on the baking sheet for 15 minutes; then place it in the center of a preheated 375-degree oven for 30 minutes or until the crust is golden. Remove from the oven and let stand for 8 minutes before transferring it onto a serving plate. Using a very sharp knife, start slicing from the middle of the roll.

PAUL PALMER'S SHRIMP TIEPIDO

ITALY

Serves 6

1½ lb shrimp, shelled (save shells), deveined
2 c water
1 c dry white wine
1 c clam juice
1 bay leaf
3 sprigs parsley
leaves from 2 celery ribs
¼ t dry thyme
½ c olive oil
2 T fresh lemon juice
1½ t salt
½ t pepper

Place the shrimp shells, water, wine, and clam juice in a saucepan. Wrap the bay leaf, parsley, celery leaves, and thyme in cheesecloth and tie it. Add to the saucepan. Simmer, uncovered, for 20 minutes. Strain the liquid into a bowl. Arrange the shrimp in one layer in a large saucepan. Pour enough of the strained liquid from the bowl over the shrimp to cover them. Bring to a boil. Remove from the heat. Cover and let the shrimp stand for 2 minutes. Meanwhile pour the olive oil and lemon juice in a bowl, add the salt and pepper, and mix well. Drain the shrimp and toss in the olive oil and lemon sauce, coating each shrimp well, and serve them warm.

SHRIMP BALLS

INDONESIA

Serves 8

1½ lb shrimp, shelled, deveined
1 (6-oz) can water chestnuts, finely minced
⅓ c finely minced scallions (white part only)
1 garlic clove, finely minced
1 egg, beaten
1½ t salt
4 t cornstarch
4 T peanut oil

Put the shrimp through the fine blade of a food grinder. Blend the ground shrimp well with chestnuts, scallions, garlic, egg, salt, and 2 teaspoons of the cornstarch. Chill for 2 hours. Form into balls the size of jumbo olives. Roll the balls lightly in the remaining cornstarch and sauté in hot peanut oil until golden. Drain on paper towels and serve either warm or cold.

SPANISH SHRIMP

Serves 6

The Spanish serve this either hot or cold. We like it hot. But on a hot summer's day, shrimp boiled briefly, cooled, and then marinated in the sauce in the refrigerator are refreshing.

1½ lb shrimp, shelled, deveined
1 c dry sherry
¼ c olive oil
4 large garlic cloves, mashed
salt and pepper to taste
2 T minced parsley

In a bowl place shrimp, sherry, olive oil, and garlic. Season with salt and pepper and blend well. Marinate for 2 hours. Discard the garlic and place the shrimp and marinade in a saucepan. Cook for about 2 minutes or just until shrimp turn pink. Do not overcook or shrimp will harden. While still heating, sprinkle with parsley. Serve the shrimp with a large spoon of the sauce in individual warmed bowls, with toast cut in strips for dunking.

TARAMASALATA

GREECE

Serves 6

⅔ c red caviar
3 small potatoes, boiled in their skins, peeled
1 small white onion, minced
juice of 1 lemon
about 1 c olive oil

The Greeks use a mortar and pestle and work the fish roe, potatoes, and onions into a paste and then thin it with lemon juice and olive oil into a smooth, thick sauce. You can lessen the effort by using a blender. If you do use a blender, add the red caviar, potatoes, and onion and whirl into a smooth paste. Then, with the blender in motion, add the lemon juice and olive oil a little at a time, until the mixture has the consistency of very thick mayonnaise. The Greeks spread it on their own flat bread and eat it while drinking pine-scented retsina wine. We like it on crackers, toast, or small thin pieces of bread. *Tarama,* a salted carp roe, is used in Greece, but we like the red caviar better as it is less pungent.

SONYA MURPHY'S WATER CHESTNUTS AND BACON

CHINA

Serves 8

The Chinese use very thin wafers of pork or sometimes chicken breast, but this version we had with Mrs. Murphy is also classic. We later had it in a Chinese home. These "chestnuts" come in two forms widely used in Asia. One is a floating aquatic plant bearing a four-pronged nutlike fruit, and the other is a Chinese grass—the corm, or bulb, of which is used. Both are available in cans in this country.

16 slices bacon
32 water chestnuts, soaked three hours in enough soy sauce to cover them

Cut the slices of bacon in half so you have 32 short slices. Wrap each half slice tightly around each water chestnut. If necessary, secure each with a toothpick. Broil until bacon is crisp. Drain on paper towels. Serve immediately.

CHAPTER TWO

Soups

A suggestion: Whenever you need an idea for a lunch or an informal supper with friends, check this chapter. The country people, farmers, fishermen–so-called peasants–generally respect soup so much that rarely do they prepare it just for a first course. For them it is a meal in a bowl. Served with crusty homemade bread, freshly churned butter, and wine from the barrel in the cellar, it is one of the important meals of the day. Of course, some of these lusty soups can be offered in small amounts as a first course, but none has such shallow character that it can't stand up on its own two feet as a superb supper.

POLISH BARLEY-MUSHROOM SOUP

Serves 6

- **2 lb shin beef on the bone**
- **3 qt water**
- **2 t salt**
- **1 t pepper**
- **3 T butter**
- **½ lb small mushrooms with stems, cleaned, thinly sliced**
- **1 c barley**

In a deep pot place the beef and bone, cover with the water, and add salt and pepper. Bring to a boil; cover the pot and simmer for 2 hours or until meat is almost cooked. Remove the beef and bone and cool. Then dice the meat and return it to the pot.

In a saucepan sauté the mushroom slices for 2 minutes in the butter. Add the mushrooms in their butter to the soup pot. Stir in the barley, cover the pot, and simmer for 15 minutes or until meat is tender and barley is cooked. Taste for seasoning.

BORSCHT

RUSSIA

Serves 6 to 8

4 (each 13¾ oz) cans of beef broth
2 cups finely shredded cabbage
4 medium-sized, white onions, finely chopped
2 large garlic cloves, minced
1 (1-lb) can tomatoes, broken up
1 small bay leaf, crumbled
2 T sugar
1 t paprika
juice of 2 lemons
grated rind of one lemon (none of the white part)
4 medium-sized, fresh beets, cooked, finely chopped
2 c beet juice (saved from cooking the beets)
3 T chopped parsley
a bowl of sour cream
salt and pepper to taste

In a large pot place beef broth, cabbage, onions, garlic, tomatoes, bay leaf, sugar, paprika, lemon juice, lemon rind. Cover the pot and simmer, stirring occasionally, for 1 hour. Add the beets and beet juice. Cook, uncovered, 10 minutes. Stir in the parsley. Bring the soup to a simmer. Serve in hot soup bowls. Pass the sour cream and salt and pepper. Borscht can also be served chilled.

FLEMISH FARMER'S SOUP

BELGIUM

Serves 6

There is a unique flavor principle involved in this soup. It is surprising the piquancy a small amount of lemon can impart to a combination of ingredients to which it seems unrelated. Also, Belgian farmers use pigeons (not squabs) for this, which add considerable flavor, but a nice stewing chicken gives almost as good a base.

1 4-lb chicken (or 2 large pigeons), cut up
1 beef shin bone
1 pork bone (not ham)
3½ qt water
2 t salt
1 t pepper
3 white onions, chopped
3 whole leeks (white and green parts), chopped
3 small carrots, scraped and chopped
3 egg yolks beaten with 1 cup whipping cream
2½ T fresh lemon juice

In a large pot place the chicken (or pigeons), beef and pork bones, the water, salt, and pepper. Bring to a boil, uncovered, and cook 10 minutes, skimming off the discolored foam that will collect on the surface. Add the onions, leeks, and carrots and simmer for 1 hour, covered, and 1½ hours partially covered, propping a wooden spoon under one side of the lid. When the bird is fork tender, remove it to cool. Take the meat from the bones and cut into pieces about 1 inch by 1 inch. Discard the beef and pork bones (save and dice any meat adhering to them) and strain the soup, pushing the vegetables through the strainer. Pour the strained broth into the soup pot, bring to a boil, and cook, uncovered, over medium heat until the liquid has been reduced almost by half. Add the chicken pieces (and any diced beef or pork), reduce to the barest simmer, and slowly stir in the beaten eggs and cream. Do not boil. Continue stirring until soup thickens; then add the lemon juice, blending it well with the soup. Taste for seasoning.

CHEESE AND POTATO SOUP

SWITZERLAND

Serves 6

3 T butter
1 T olive oil
2 small white onions, diced
1 garlic clove, minced
2 medium-sized leeks (white part only), diced
4 small new potatoes, peeled, diced
2 c chicken broth
2 c medium cream
2 c milk
⅓ c grated Parmesan cheese
salt and pepper to taste
2 c grated Gruyère cheese
2 T chopped parsley

In a deep pot heat the butter and oil. Add onion, garlic, and leeks and sauté until they are soft. Add potatoes and chicken broth and bring to a boil. Reduce heat and simmer until the potatoes are cooked (about 15 minutes). Stir in the cream, milk, and the Parmesan cheese. Bring soup to just under a boil. Reduce heat and keep at a simmer and stir in salt and pepper to taste (remembering that cheese is salty). Stir the grated Gruyère cheese into the hot soup 5 minutes before serving (or long enough before to melt cheese). Sprinkle with parsley.

CODFISH SOUP

SPAIN

Serves 6

3 T olive oil
2 onions, thinly sliced
2 garlic cloves, minced
1½ lb codfish steaks
1 (1-lb) can tomatoes, broken up
2 c clam juice
1 c water
3 T chopped parsley
½ t powdered saffron
1 t salt
½ t pepper
rind (not white part) of ½ lemon and ½ orange, cut into thin strips

In a large pot heat the oil and sauté onions and garlic until they are soft. Push onions and garlic to one side and sauté the codfish steaks for 3 minutes on each side. Add the tomatoes, clam juice, water, parsley, saffron, salt, and pepper. Bring to a boil, cover, and simmer for 20 minutes (or until fish flakes with a fork but is still firm). Remove fish and cool. Stir in the strips of lemon and orange rind; simmer, uncovered, 7 minutes. Pick skin and bones from cod. Cut meat into small chunks and return to soup pot. Simmer 5 minutes. Taste for seasoning.

FISKESUPPE

SCANDINAVIA

Serves 6

This, or a dish very similar to it, is standard country fare in seagirt Scandinavia. We first had this lusty dish made with startlingly fresh young cod, "scrod," aboard the *Havella,* a diesel ketch, cruising the Arctic Ocean off the Norwegian archipelago, Spitsbergen. First, you make the fish stock.

Stock

trimmings from a cleaned scrod (head, tail, fins, bones)
2 small onions, chopped
2 small carrots, scraped and chopped
3 medium-sized potatoes, peeled, chopped
1 t salt
½ t pepper
1 small bay leaf, crumbled
4 small celery ribs with leaves, scraped and chopped
3 qt water

Combine all the ingredients in a large pot. Bring to a boil; then simmer, uncovered, for 45 minutes. Strain the liquid. Discard the fish parts. Push the vegetables through a strainer and return the liquid and strained vegetables to the pot.

Fish Soup

½ c minced turnips
½ c minced white onions
⅓ c minced carrots
2 lb scrod fillets in large pieces
2 egg yolks
salt and pepper to taste
6 heaping T sour cream

Over high heat reduce the strained stock to about 8 cups. Add the turnips, onions, and carrots to the reduced stock. Simmer, uncovered, for 10 minutes. Add the fish; simmer 10 minutes. Remove the fish. In a bowl beat the egg yolks with 4 tablespoons of the hot soup, adding one tablespoon of soup at a time.

Remove soup pot from the heat and add egg yolk mixture, stirring vigorously until it is well blended. Cut the fish into ½-inch cubes; stir them into the soup. Season. Reheat slowly, but do not bring near a simmer or the egg will curdle. Serve in deep bowls with a dollop of sour cream on top. Coarse, dark bread, spread with sweet butter, and beer usually accompany this supper-in-a-soup-bowl.

GARLIC SOUP

FRANCE

Serves 6

2½ qt chicken broth
20 large garlic cloves, peeled, cut in halves
salt and pepper to taste
½ c arrowroot
5 T water
6 egg yolks
12 ½-inch-thick slices French bread fried in butter until golden on both sides and drained on paper towel

Bring the chicken broth to a boil. Add the garlic. Reduce the heat, cover, and simmer 45 minutes. Discard the garlic. Season with salt and pepper. Blend the arrowroot with the water into a smooth mixture and stir it into the chicken broth. Beat the egg yolks in a bowl; then slowly stir into them 2 cups of the broth. Remove the soup pot from the heat and slowly stir this egg yolk mixture into it. Return to low heat and with a wire whisk, beat the eggs into the broth until it has thickened. Do not bring near a simmer or the egg yolks will curdle. Taste for seasoning. Place 2 slices of the fried bread in the bottom of each bowl. Ladle the soup over the bread and serve immediately as the arrowroot does not hold together too long.

GAZPACHO

SPAIN

Serves 6

This is a tangy, zesty, countryman's soup that we have had in various versions in farm kitchens and numerous restaurants. This is the one that we prefer, obtained from the chef of our friend Antonio Fernandez in his restaurant in Madrid, Botin, which many claim is one of the best restaurants in Europe. It is a soup served in summer and is at its best very cold.

5 large ripe tomatoes, peeled, seeded, coarsely chopped
1 medium-sized white onion, coarsely chopped
1 garlic clove, cut in half
2 c cold beef bouillon
2 T olive oil
2 T wine vinegar
1 t salt
¼ t black pepper
¼ t paprika
4 oz dry sherry
½ c fine bread crumbs
1 c finely chopped cucumber
1 c finely chopped green pepper
1 c finely chopped white onion
a bowl of garlic croutons

Combine all of the ingredients through the paprika. Refrigerate for 2 hours. Pour into a blender jar and blend for 1½ minutes. Pour into a bowl and stir in the sherry and bread crumbs. Ladle the soup into chilled soup bowls; add one ice cube to each bowl. Place the chopped cucumbers, peppers, onions, and croutons in separate bowls on the table and encourage your guests to add their own selections to the soup.

LENTIL SOUP

Serves 6

This is popular in many places in Europe. The Germans claim it, as do the Hungarians, Bulgarians, Austrians, Swiss, Poles, Russians, and some Italians. So do we.

1 c dry lentils
2 T butter
5 slices lean, thick-cut bacon, finely diced
2 small white onions, thinly sliced
2 small carrots, scraped, thinly sliced
1 ham bone (left over from that baked ham)
1 qt beef broth
water the lentils soaked in
3 small new potatoes, peeled, thinly sliced
1 small bay leaf
pinch of marjoram
salt and pepper to taste
2 knockwurst, skinned, cut into ¼-inch slices
2 c medium cream

Pick over the lentils and rinse them several times; cover them well with water and soak for 5 hours. Melt butter in a large pot and sauté the bacon and onions until both are soft. Add the carrots, the ham bone, lentils and the water they soaked in, and the beef broth. Cover the pot and simmer for 1 hour. Add the potatoes, bay leaf, and marjoram. Simmer, covered, for 30 minutes. Season with salt and pepper. Add the knockwurst slices and continue simmering, uncovered, for 10 minutes. Stir the cream into the hot soup, heat to just below a boil, and serve.

MINESTRONE MARIA LUISA

ITALY

Serves 8

Anyone who doesn't like this soup gets his money back.—J.D.S.

½ c dried chick-peas, soaked 5 hours, drained
½ c dried white kidney beans, soaked 5 hours, drained
2½ qt beef broth (we use homemade, with little nuggets of beef)
3 T olive oil
2 white onions, chopped
2 garlic cloves, minced
1 (1-lb) can tomatoes, broken up
½ c cabbage, chopped
½ c carrot, chopped
½ c celery, chopped
⅓ c ditalini (little pasta thimbles), cooked al dente, drained
1½ t salt
½ t pepper
pinch of crushed, dried red pepper
1 c grated Parmesan cheese

In a large pot place chick-peas and beans; pour in the beef broth, bring to a boil, and simmer, covered, for 40 minutes. In a saucepan heat the oil and sauté the onions and garlic until soft. Stir in the tomatoes; simmer 15 minutes. In a small pot cook the cabbage, carrots, and celery in salted water until slightly underdone; drain well. Stir the tomatoes, vegetables, and the cooked pasta into the bean pot. Season with salt, pepper, and red pepper; stir well and simmer, uncovered, for 10 minutes. Taste for seasoning. Serve in large soup bowls with Parmesan cheese sprinkled on top. Plenty of bread and chilled wine won't hurt the guests' feelings.

MULLIGATAWNY

ENGLAND

Serves 8 to 10

1 (3½-lb) chicken, cut up
4 qt water
3 small white onions, quartered
leaves from 3 celery ribs, chopped
4 juniper berries
1 t salt
½ t pepper
3 small carrots, scraped and cut into small dices
1 small green pepper, seeds and white part removed, cut into small dices
4 small white onions, chopped
3 celery ribs, scraped, chopped
1 medium-sized, tart apple, peeled, cored, and chopped
2 T cornstarch
1 T curry powder
¾ c broth from stewing chicken
1 T sugar
½ t ground cumin
½ t yellow mustard seed
pinch of nutmeg
4 T minced parsley

In a large pot place the cut-up chicken and cover with the water; add the onions, celery leaves, juniper berries; season with salt and pepper. Cover the pot and simmer the chicken for 1 hour or until the bird is fork tender. Remove the chicken to cool. Strain the stock; then return it to the pot. Add the carrots, green pepper, onion, and celery. Simmer, uncovered, for 30 minutes. Stir in the apple. Cook for 10 minutes. Combine the cornstarch and curry powder in a small bowl. Stirring steadily, add to the bowl ¾ cup of broth from the chicken pot, making a smooth paste. Stir this into the soup pot, along with the sugar, cumin, mustard seed, and nutmeg. Mix well and bring to a simmer. Meanwhile, remove the meat from the chicken pieces and discard skin and bones. Dice the chicken and stir it into the pot. Taste for seasoning. Serve in hot bowls, sprinkled with parsley.

ONION SOUP

FRANCE

Serves 6

5 T butter
2 T olive oil
2½ lb yellow onions, thinly sliced
1 t salt
½ t pepper
4 T flour
1 qt beef broth
1 qt chicken broth

In a large pot heat the butter and oil; add onions, salt, and pepper and sauté until onions are golden. Sprinkle the flour over the onions, stir it in well, and cook for 5 minutes. Add the beef and chicken broth, stir well, and bring to a boil. Then reduce heat and simmer, covered, for 50 minutes. Taste for seasoning. In France the soup is usually served floating croutons lavishly sprinkled with grated cheese and run under the broiler until the cheese has melted. You can buy croutons, or you can fry small pieces of French bread in olive oil and garlic until crusty brown on each side and then drain them on a paper towel.

PASTINA ALLA TOSCANA

ITALY

Serves 6 to 8

2 T olive oil
4 T butter
1 lb beef round, cut into pieces half the size of your thumbnail
2 small yellow onions, chopped
1 T minced Italian parsley
3 fresh basil leaves, minced
4 large, ripe tomatoes, peeled and chopped
2 qt chicken broth
salt and pepper to taste
½ c uncooked spinach, coarsely chopped
½ c uncooked escarole, coarsely chopped
5 chicken livers, coarsely chopped
3 T pastina (a very small pasta for soups)

In a large pot heat the oil and 2 tablespoons of the butter; add beef and onions and sauté for 10 minutes. Stir in the parsley, basil, tomatoes, chicken broth, salt, and pepper. Simmer for 30 minutes, uncovered. Stir in the spinach and escarole; simmer for 15 minutes. In a frying pan heat the remaining butter, add the chicken livers, and sauté for 4 minutes. Add the chicken livers and *pastina* to the pot; stir and simmer for 10 minutes or until *pastina* is cooked. Taste for seasoning.

PEA SOUP

GERMANY

Serves 6 to 8

This soup needs a ham bone with some ham remaining on it. No self-respecting peasant ever throws any kind of bone away.

1½ lb dry, green or yellow split peas, picked over and rinsed several times
4 qt water
1 ham bone
3 medium-sized carrots, scraped and chopped
3 medium-sized onions, chopped
4 celery ribs, scraped and chopped
salt and pepper to taste
1 c medium cream

In a large pot soak the peas in the water for 4 hours. Add the ham bone, carrots, onions, celery, salt, and pepper to the pot. Bring to a boil; then simmer, covered, for 2½ hours or until the peas are soft and the soup thickens. Remove the ham bone to cool. Put everything else in the soup pot through a food mill. Return the puree to the pot. Remove bits of ham from the bone and add them and the cream to the soup. Bring the soup to a simmer, taste for seasoning, and serve immediately.

PISTOU

FRANCE

Serves 8

This soup is guaranteed to make your taste buds tango. The combination of flavors and textures is unique. First, make the *pistou.*

½ c olive oil	**7 cloves garlic**
¾ c tangy, grated cheese (we like Parmesan)	**5 large, fresh basil leaves**

Combine all the ingredients and with a mortar and pestle work into a smooth paste or use a blender. Set mixture aside.

1 lb pea beans, picked over, soaked 5 hours, drained	**3 large, ripe tomatoes, peeled, seeded, chopped**
4 qt water	**3 small fresh leaves of sage**
2 new potatoes, diced	**1½ t salt**
½ lb fresh, young, yellow string beans, diced	**½ t pepper**
4 leeks, white part only, diced	**6 oz vermicelli (a fine pasta)**
4 small zucchini, unpeeled, diced	

In a large pot place the beans with the water; bring to a boil, cover, and simmer for 40 minutes. Add the potatoes, string beans, leeks, zucchini, tomatoes, sage, salt, and pepper. Simmer 1 hour or until vegetables are tender. Stir in the *vermicelli;* cook, uncovered, for 10 minutes or until the pasta is cooked. Just before serving stir in the *pistou* paste.

PETITE MARMITE

FRANCE

Serves 6

This family supper soup is named for the earthenware pot (*marmite*) in which it is cooked. But any deep soup pot will do.

1 lb lean beef—top round, shoulder, or brisket—trimmed of all fat and cut into 2-inch cubes
1 (3-lb) chicken, cut up
2 qt beef broth
1 qt chicken broth
bouquet garni (1 bay leaf, 2 sprigs of parsley, pinch of thyme tied in a cheesecloth)
1 carrot, coarsely chopped
1 celery rib, coarsely chopped
1 yellow onion stuck with 2 cloves
salt and pepper to taste
12 pieces of carrot cut into the size and shape of large olives
12 pieces of turnip cut same way as carrots
1 c coarsely chopped cabbage
3 leeks, white part only, cut into 1-inch-long pieces
12 pieces potato cut same way as carrots
6 1-inch-long pieces of marrow bone wrapped in cheesecloth
3 slices bread, cut ½ inch thick, crusts removed, each slice cut into 4 diamonds and fried in butter until golden on both sides, drained on paper towels
grated Parmesan cheese

In a large pot cover the beef and chicken with water. Cover the pot, bring to a boil, and simmer for 2 minutes. Drain, discard the water, and rinse the beef and chicken under cold water to remove all scum. Rinse pot. Return beef to the pot and pour in the beef broth and chicken broth. Add the bouquet garni, carrot, celery, onion stuck with cloves, salt, and pepper. Simmer, uncovered, for 1 hour. Add the chicken and simmer until beef and chicken are tender. (If the chicken becomes tender before the beef does, remove it.) When meats are tender, cut the beef into pieces 1 inch square and ¼ inch thick. Remove and discard the skin from the chicken and cut the choice pieces as you did the beef. (The rest of the chicken can be used for something else.) Strain the broth, return it to the pot, and cook the pieces of carrots, turnips, cabbage, and leeks for 10 minutes; add potatoes and cook, uncovered, until all vegetables are tender. Add beef and chicken; simmer 3 minutes. Taste for seasoning. Meanwhile, simmer the marrow bones in 2 cups of the broth for ½ hour. At serving time remove cheesecloth and place one piece of marrow bone in the bottom of fairly large soup bowls. Ladle in the broth, meat, and vegetables and serve very hot with the fried bread and Parmesan cheese. If you have individual earthenware soup bowls, it is good to float 2 croutons on top, sprinkle with Parmesan cheese, and put each bowl under the broiler until the cheese melts and is golden.

SAUSAGE AND PASTA SOUP

ITALY

Serves 6 to 8

- **½ lb pea beans, picked over, soaked 5 hours, drained**
- **3 qt chicken broth**
- **2 T olive oil**
- **3 hot Italian sausages, pricked in several places**
- **3 sweet Italian sausages, pricked in several places**
- **3 small potatoes, diced**
- **1 carrot, scraped, chopped**
- **2 small white onions, chopped**
- **2 small celery ribs, chopped**
- **4 ripe tomatoes, peeled, seeded, diced**
- **salt and pepper to taste**
- **1 c cravatte (bow ties) or your choice of small pasta, cooked al dente (still chewy)**

In a large pot place the beans and cover with 2 quarts of the chicken broth. Cover the pot, bring it to a boil, and simmer for 1 hour. Meanwhile, in another pot heat the oil and sauté the sausages, browning them evenly. Pour off all but 2 T fat. Add the potatoes, carrot, onions, celery, tomatoes, salt, and pepper. Cover the pot and simmer, stirring, for 15 minutes. Remove the sausages; cut them into ¼-inch rounds. Return the sausage to the pot; pour in the remaining chicken broth and simmer, uncovered, 20 minutes. Add the contents of this pot to the simmering bean pot. Stir the pasta into the bean pot and simmer, uncovered, for 5 minutes. Taste for seasoning.

SCOTCH BROTH

Serves 6

In Scotland, mutton is used, but that is a bit gamey and hard to get here, and lamb does the job just as well. Have your butcher bone a leg of lamb. You need the bone. Then trim the stewing parts from the leg. These are the less lean, less perfect pieces of lamb. You need 2 pounds for the soup.

bone from the lamb leg
2 lb lamb, cut into large cubes
leaves from 3 ribs of celery, chopped
3 medium-sized onions, cut up
1 bay leaf, crumbled
4 cloves
3 qt cold water
salt and pepper to taste
3 small carrots, scraped, diced
3 celery ribs, scraped, diced
4 small scallions, chopped (do not use green part)
¾ c barley
3 T chopped parsley

In a deep pot place the lamb bone, the pieces of lamb, celery leaves, onions, bay leaf, and cloves. Cover with the cold water and season with salt and pepper. Simmer, covered, for 1½ hours or until the lamb is fork tender, removing the scum from the top from time to time. Remove the meat to cool. Strain the liquid. Return it to the pot and add the carrots, celery, scallions, and barley. Simmer, uncovered, for 30 minutes or until vegetables and barley are cooked. Dice the lamb and add it to the pot. Stir well; taste for seasoning. Serve in bowls and sprinkle with the parsley.

TOMATO EGG DROP SOUP

CHINA

Serves 6

2 qt rich chicken broth
1 (1-lb) can stewed tomatoes, mashed into small pieces
2 T cornstarch, blended with ¼ cup cold water
3 eggs, beaten
4 tender scallions, chopped (use all parts)

In a large pot bring the broth to a boil; add tomatoes. When the mixture boils again, stir in the cornstarch. Reduce heat and stir until the soup thickens. Then slowly stir the beaten eggs into the now simmering soup. When all of the eggs have been stirred in, remove the soup from the heat. Serve immediately, sprinkled with the raw, chopped scallions.

ZUCCHINI, LEEK, AND POTATO SOUP

BULGARIA

Serves 6

4 leeks, white part only, cut in half lengthwise, then into ½-inch pieces
1 large carrot, scraped, cut into ¼-inch cubes
1 stick butter
6 c chicken broth
2 medium-sized potatoes, cut into ½-inch cubes
salt and pepper to taste
3 very small zucchini, cut in half lengthwise, then into ½-inch-thick pieces
2 T chopped fresh dill (or parsley)

In a large pot simmer the leeks and carrot in the butter until they are well coated–about 5 minutes. Add the broth, potatoes, salt, and pepper. Bring to a boil; then simmer, covered, about 30 minutes or until the potatoes are slightly undercooked. Stir in the zucchini and simmer for 20 minutes or until the potato and zucchini are tender. Taste for seasoning. Serve with the dill (or parsley) sprinkled on top.

ZUPPA ALLA PAESANA

ITALY

Serves 6

1 lb dried lentils, rinsed, soaked in water for 5 hours, drained
1 T olive oil
1 T butter
8 anchovies, drained, mashed
2 celery ribs (with leaves), scraped and chopped
1 garlic clove, minced
1 T chopped broad-leafed parsley
4 large, ripe tomatoes, peeled, diced
1 qt water
1 qt chicken broth
salt and pepper to taste
½ c maruzzine (small pasta snail shells), cooked al dente
grated Parmesan cheese

Cover the lentils with water and simmer, covered, for 1 hour or until they are tender. In a large pot heat the oil and butter; stir in the anchovies, celery, garlic, and parsley. Sauté until the celery is soft. Stir in the tomatoes; add the water, broth, and some pepper. Bring to a boil; then simmer, uncovered, for 25 minutes. Stir the lentils and their cooking liquid into the soup; simmer for 10 minutes. Add the pasta shells; stir well. Taste for seasoning. Serve in bowls with the Parmesan cheese sprinkled on top.

CHAPTER THREE

Eggs

"Which came first, the chicken or the egg?" is not a question pondered by the peasant. If he doesn't walk out to the barnyard to get eggs so fresh that the hens are still clucking over their depository victory, he barters for or buys them in an open market from other farmers who believe it sinful to trade in eggs over a day old. And the peasant can do as much with the egg as he can with the chicken.

For farm folk, especially in Europe, eggs are not merely a breakfast food or something to fluff up for lunch in a fancy omelette. Eggs are treated with as much respect as meat, as an important food around which a meal is built. Sure, peasants do make omelettes, but they are far from ordinary, containing enough ingredients to make them a complete meal in themselves. And normally they are served thick and flat and take no particular expertise or special pans. Try eating eggs melded with potatoes, ham, peppers, onions, or various other combinations, and you'll have no doubts about eggs being important as meal mainstays.

And who other than country folk, with their respect for the versatility of eggs, would think of poaching them in red wine or tomatoes? But, enough. Recipes follow our ode to the egg and to the peasant whose imagination created this chapter.

BASQUE PIPÉRADE

Serves 6

The Basques, an uncommunicative people of unknown origin whose language seems to have no relationship to any other, inhabit the western Pyrenees Mountains of France and Spain. Wearing floppy berets even at the table and living in whitewashed farmhouses, they are famous for their simple but imaginative food and their skill at the game of pelota. We like what they do with ham and eggs.

3 T butter
3 T olive oil
½ c green peppers, seeds and white part removed, thinly sliced
½ c red peppers, seeds and white part removed, thinly sliced
1 clove garlic, chopped
½ c white onions, thinly sliced
1 c cooked ham, cut into small dices
2 tomatoes, peeled, seeded, coarsely chopped
salt and pepper to taste
9 eggs, beaten
3 anchovy fillets, drained, cut into thin strips

In a frying pan heat the butter and oil. Add the green and red peppers, garlic, and onions, sautéing until the vegetables are soft. Stir in the ham and the tomatoes and season with salt and pepper; stir well and simmer, uncovered, for 15 minutes or until most of the liquid from the tomatoes has cooked off. Mix the anchovies with the eggs; stir them into the vegetable mixture. Raise heat, scrambling eggs until firm. This is a fast operation taking a minute. Stop stirring and lower heat; cook for about 3 minutes or until the bottom of the omelette is well set. Give the pan several hearty shakes or use a spatula to loosen the *pipérade;* then slide it out onto a warm platter like a cake.

EGGS WITH CHICKEN LIVERS

GREECE

Serves 6

- 8 T (1 stick) butter
- 3 small white onions, finely chopped
- ½ lb chicken livers, diced
- 8 eggs
- salt and pepper to taste

In a large frying pan melt 4 tablespoons of the butter and sauté the onions until they are soft. Add the livers and cook 4 minutes. In a large bowl beat the eggs with salt and pepper until frothy. Melt the remaining butter in the frying pan with the onions and livers, pour in the eggs, and cook over medium heat, stirring constantly for 5 minutes or until the eggs are set but still creamy. Do not overcook.

EGGS POACHED IN RED WINE

FRANCE

Serves 4

- 4 slices bread, cut about ⅜ inch thick, crusts removed, rubbed with a cut clove of garlic and fried in butter on both sides until golden, drained on paper towels
- 8 medium-sized mushrooms, stems removed but saved
- 5 T butter
- 3 c dry red wine
- 1 c chicken broth
- 1 celery rib, chopped
- 4 shallots, chopped
- 1 bay leaf
- 1 lump of sugar
- pinch of dry thyme
- salt and pepper to taste
- 8 eggs
- 3 T butter kneaded with 2 T flour
- 2 T parsley, chopped

Prepare the bread; keep warm. Sauté the mushrooms in 2 tablespoons of the butter until they brown. Do not overcook them; they should be tender but firm. In a saucepan combine the wine, broth, celery, mushroom stems, shallots, bay leaf, sugar, thyme, salt, and pepper; simmer for 25 minutes, uncovered. Strain the liquid and return it to the saucepan. Bring it to a boil.

Break the eggs, one at a time, into a saucer and slip them into the liquid. Poach two or three eggs (or whatever number can be poached at one time without crowding) until the whites are firm. Remove the eggs with a slotted spoon and keep them warm while the others are poaching. After all of the eggs have been removed from the saucepan, add the kneaded butter to the wine sauce and simmer, stirring, until the sauce thickens. Taste for seasoning. Arrange the warm fried bread on a hot serving dish, place 2 eggs on each slice of bread, then a mushroom on each egg. Stir 3 tablespoons of butter into the thickened sauce and spoon it over the mushrooms and eggs. Sprinkle with parsley.

MARIA CIFELLI LIMONCELLI'S EGGS POACHED IN TOMATO SAUCE

ITALY

Serves 6

1 small onion, chopped
1 garlic clove, minced
3 T olive oil
1 (1-lb, 12-oz) can tomatoes, broken up
salt and pepper to taste
pinch of marjoram
1 T chopped parsley
6 eggs

In a frying pan sauté the onion and garlic in the oil until they are golden. Add the tomatoes; season with salt and pepper; add marjoram and parsley. Simmer until the sauce thickens and most of the watery content has cooked off. Break eggs, separately, into a small bowl; then slip them into the sauce and simmer until the whites are firmly set. Serve with some good crusty bread to dip into the sauce.

EGG AND POTATO PUDDING

CZECHOSLOVAKIA

Serves 6

4 large potatoes, peeled, finely grated
3 small white onions, finely grated
4 eggs, beaten
2 T minced parsley
1½ t salt
½ t pepper
2 T melted butter mixed with 1 T olive oil

Oil a ring mold large enough to hold all ingredients. Place the potatoes in a strainer for 5 minutes to let any excess water drain off. In a large bowl combine the potatoes, onions, eggs, parsley, salt, and pepper. Mix well. Spoon the mixture into the ring mold. Dribble the melted butter and oil over the top. Set on a baking sheet and bake in a preheated 400-degree oven for 1 hour or until the top forms a golden crust. Loosen sides with a spatula and invert on a warm serving platter. The center of the mold can be filled with any variety of creamed vegetables. We like a mixture of creamed spinach and mushrooms. Or the pudding can be served in thick slices as it is.

EGG AND SAUSAGE CAKE

HUNGARY

Serves 6

8 T (1 stick) butter
4 T olive oil
3 medium-sized potatoes, cut into ⅛-inch-thick slices
2 t salt
4 small white onions, chopped
3 hot Italian sausages, pricked, parboiled 5 minutes, then broiled 10 minutes, and sliced into ⅛-inch-thick rounds
5 eggs

In a large frying pan heat 5 tablespoons of the butter and 2 tablespoons of the oil. Place the potatoes into the hot fat, and turning them several times until they are well coated with fat, sprinkle with 1 teaspoon of the salt. Cook over medium heat for 10 minutes until potatoes are browned lightly. Push potatoes to one side in the pan, add the onions, and cook for 5 minutes. Mix potatoes and onions and sausage together and cook 5 minutes. Transfer the potatoes, onions, and sausage to a strainer to drain off the fat. Break the eggs into a bowl, add remaining salt, and beat into a froth. Stir the drained potatoes, onions, and sausage into the eggs. Heat the remaining butter and oil in an 8-inch frying pan. When very hot, pour in the egg mixture, spreading it so it will cook evenly over medium heat. From time to time take the pan off the heat and give it a vigorous shake to prevent the eggs from sticking. When the eggs become firm (in about 4 minutes), remove from the heat and place a plate over the pan. Holding the pan handle with one hand and the plate with the other, turn the egg cake onto the plate; runny, uncooked side will be down. Slide it from the plate back into the frying pan and cook 3 minutes. Serve.

EGGS WITH SCALLIONS

BULGARIA

Serves 6

5 T butter
1 T olive oil
10 young scallions (white and green parts), chopped

4 T flour
8 eggs
1 c medium cream
1½ t salt
3 T chopped parsley

In a large frying pan heat the butter and oil. Sauté the scallions until they are soft. Sprinkle with the flour and cook, stirring, until the flour is light brown. Beat the eggs, cream, and salt together. Stir the egg-cream mixture into the frying pan, blending it well with the flour and onions. Cook over medium heat, stirring into a soft scramble (about 5 minutes). Sprinkle with the parsley.

EGG SCRAPPLE

GERMANY

Serves 6

- **4 T butter**
- **1 T olive oil**
- **2 small white onions, chopped**
- **1 small green pepper, seeds and white part removed, diced**
- **4 small potatoes, peeled, diced**
- **1 t salt**
- **½ t pepper**
- **1 medium-sized, fresh ripe tomato, peeled, seeded, diced**
- **6 eggs, separated**

In a large shallow top-of-stove-to-oven pan, heat the butter and oil over medium heat; sauté onions and pepper until they are soft. Stir in the potatoes; season with salt and pepper. Cover pan and simmer for 15 minutes. Blend the tomato with vegetables. Place egg yolks in one bowl, whites in another. Beat the yolks until they are light and frothy. Beat the whites stiff. Fold the whites into the yolks; then blend the eggs with the tomato mixture. Cover the pan and bake in a preheated 350-degree oven for 20 minutes or until the top is golden brown and the eggs are set.

EGGS WITH VEGETABLES

YUGOSLAVIA

Serves 6

- **4 T butter**
- **2 T olive oil**
- **2 medium-sized green peppers, seeds and white part removed, finely chopped**
- **2 very small peperonis (hot peppers), seeds and white part removed, finely chopped**
- **4 small white onions, finely chopped**
- **2 medium-sized ripe tomatoes, peeled, seeded, cut into eighths**
- **8 eggs, beaten**
- **¾ c cottage cheese, well drained**
- **1 t salt**

In a large frying pan heat 2 tablespoons of the butter and 1 of the oil. Sauté the green peppers until they are almost soft. Add remaining butter and oil, the *peperonis,* onions, and tomatoes; simmer for 10 minutes until tomato liquid is almost gone. Add the beaten eggs and cheese, sprinkle the salt, and scramble the eggs, stirring for 5 minutes. They should be soft but firm.

MARIA CIFELLI LIMONCELLI'S FRITTATA

ITALY

Serves 6

Maria Cifelli Limoncelli, our mother and mother-in-law who was the mistress and magician in the kitchen, could make you believe that an onion smelled sweeter than a rose and that a cabbage was for kings. If ten people unexpectedly dropped in at dinner time as a "surprise for Maria" as is an old Italian custom, she was never caught short; her genius made the pasta sauce grow, the chicken sprout four legs, the salad stretch bountifully. Her beautiful face flushed, more with the heat of her hospitality than from that of the kitchen, she always radiated an infectious happiness that lasted long after you left her table. Even though she is gone, the happiness stays with us today because she taught us the true meaning of the word. Enjoy the simple things, she said. Her *frittata* was one of those simple things.

4 T olive oil
2 T butter
5 small white onions, sliced wafer thin
8 eggs
4 T grated Parmesan cheese
salt and pepper to taste

In a large frying pan heat 2 tablespoons of the oil and 1 of the butter and sauté the onions until they are soft. Remove the onions and place in a strainer to drain the fat. In a large bowl beat the eggs, cheese, salt, and pepper with a fork. Add the drained onions and mix well. Heat remaining butter and oil in the large frying pan, pour in the egg mixture, and cook for 5 minutes or until the bottom and sides are set. Loosen with a spatula, and with a plate on top of the pan, flip the *frittata* onto the plate with the uncooked side down. Slide back into frying pan and cook 4 minutes until the bottom is set. Serve immediately with small boiled potatoes and mustard on the side.

Maria varied her *frittate* in interesting ways–sometimes by using chopped, ripe fresh tomato cooked in butter for 10 minutes and then drained or by adding diced leftover meats and vegetables. Three classics of hers were *frittate* with sliced young zucchini; with tender young fresh broccoli, cooked, then added; and with chicken livers. Try them all, using the basic recipe above, then adding the other cooked items of your choice. Her *frittata* is also superb with fresh spinach–washed, dried, chopped coarsely, and beaten into the raw eggs.

MEXICAN EGGS

Serves 6

4 T butter
1 medium-sized, yellow onion, finely chopped
1 large, ripe tomato, peeled, seeded, and chopped
1 t chili powder
1 T chopped parsley
12 eggs, beaten with 6 T cream and salt and pepper

In a frying pan melt butter. Sauté the onion until soft. Stir in the chopped tomato and chili powder and simmer until all the water from the tomato has cooked off. Stir in the parsley; then pour in the egg-cream mixture and stir gently, letting the uncooked part of the egg work its way to the bottom of the pan. Continue in this manner until the eggs are set but not dry.

PORTUGUESE POACHED EGGS

Serves 6

3 T butter
1 T olive oil
3 small white onions, chopped
1 c beef broth
2 c fresh small peas, cooked but still firm (or a package of frozen small peas, defrosted but not cooked)
2 ripe tomatoes, peeled, seeded, chopped
1 t salt
½ t pepper
6 small smoked garlic sausages, such as Spanish chorizo, cut into ¼-inch-thick rounds
6 jumbo eggs

In a large frying pan heat butter and oil and sauté onions until they are soft. Add the beef broth, peas, tomatoes, salt, and pepper. Stud the sausage rounds throughout the pan, burying them somewhat in the sauce. Bring sauce to a boil, cover pan, reduce to a simmer, and cook for 12 minutes. Break the eggs, separately, into a small bowl, sliding each into the sauce. Cover the pan and simmer for 5 minutes or until the whites are set. Serve each egg on a mound of the sauce.

SCRAMBLED EGGS WITH SHRIMP

CHINA

Serves 6

Here is a quick, delicious luncheon dish shared with a fisherman's family on a boat in the crowded boat city in Hong Kong.

10 eggs, lightly beaten
8 scallions (white and green parts), chopped
2 t salt
6 T peanut oil
1 lb (about 28) small shrimps, shelled, deveined, each shrimp cut into 3 pieces

In a bowl combine the eggs, chopped scallions, salt, and 2 tablespoons of oil. Blend well. Heat remaining oil in a wok or a heavy frying pan. Stir-fry the shrimp 10 seconds or until they start to turn pink; lower heat. Pour the egg mixture over them; stir gently, letting the uncooked part of the eggs work its way to the bottom of the pan. Continue in this manner until the eggs are set.

SPANISH EGG WEDGES

Serves 6

Our nine-year-old fishing guides (whom we had to pick up and carry across the streams) in Spain brought this unusual egg dish along for their lunch. They gave us each a wedge, so delicious that it made our ham sandwiches taste like sawdust in comparison.

4 T olive oil
8 eggs
salt and pepper to taste
3 medium-sized potatoes, boiled in their skins, cooled, peeled, diced
4 green olives, sliced
2 large pimiento strips, diced

In a 9-inch frying pan heat the oil. Beat the eggs until fluffy, seasoning well with salt and pepper. Pour into the hot oil. Cook 5 minutes and lay plate over pan and invert so eggs on runny side are down; slide back into the frying pan. Cook on the other side 4 minutes. Evenly spread the potatoes, olives, and pimientos over the egg cake. Fold over once, pressing the sides of the warm egg cake together (like an egg sandwich with the egg on the outside). Place on a plate and refrigerate for 3 hours. Serve cold, cut into wedges. This, called a *tortilla de patata,* can be varied and served hot. In this popular version the olives and pimientos are not used and the potatoes are cut into thin rounds and cooked for 15 minutes in oil with onions. The oil is drained from the potatoes and onions and they are blended with the beaten eggs; then the flat omelette is fried brown and puffy on both sides in the remaining oil. We like it. But memory makes that cold tortilla our favorite.

STEAMED EGGS WITH PORK AND WATER CHESTNUTS

CHINA

Serves 6

This is a well-known dish in rural China, involving cooking by steaming. Chinese steamers are available in many places, but you can make do without one. The idea: the food to be cooked is placed in an uncovered bowl. This is put into a pan holding about 1½ inches of water. The pan is covered tightly and the water brought to a vigorous boil; then the heat is reduced and the food in the open bowl is cooked by the steam flowing around it. Simply take a pot large enough to hold the bowl in which you will cook the food. Put the 1½ inches of hot water in the pot; place a wire cake rack in the water to hold the bowl with the food high enough above it so the water will not get into the food when it boils. We sometimes use a small bowl to elevate the food dish.

8 eggs, lightly beaten
½ lb very lean fresh pork, chopped
8 water chestnuts, chopped
2 small white onions, minced
4 young scallions (white and green parts), chopped
½ c chicken broth
3 T soy sauce
1½ T peanut oil
1½ t sugar
½ t salt

In a large bowl combine and blend well all ingredients. Pour into a bowl deep enough to allow the egg mixture to expand an inch as it cooks. Put the bowl in the steamer as described, with the water boiling. Cover the steamer tightly. Reduce the heat to slightly below medium and steam for 40 minutes or until eggs are set. Eggs may be steamed this way with a number of other ingredients: flaked fish, chopped bacon, chopped shrimp, chopped mushrooms, chopped ham, bamboo shoots. Or dream up your own combinations.

CHAPTER FOUR

Fish

The torches flickered on the dark sea like giant fireflies. It was almost dawn and the fishing fleet was returning to Lesbos, the Greek island where Homer stood and brooded on that "wine dark sea" over the fact that Turkey was so close that it could be clearly seen on a fair day. We, too, have stood on the shores of that seldom visited island at dawn and watched the fishing fleet return—the boats old, their once gay paints faded and flaking; the fishermen weary; the townspeople watching silently. Too often the boats returned after a long, hard night on a rough sea, with not enough fish to even feed the fishermen.

We also have stood on beaches on the Italian Riviera at dawn and watched Italian fishermen hand-haul nets in from a snarling winter sea, with so few fish netted that it was almost a useless operation. The hauling caused the muscles on the fishermen's arms to pop out like knotted cords. We have gone out with the fishermen of Marbella off the Spanish coast. We were glad to get ashore at dawn—cold, shivering, and somewhat frightened by the experience of the old, frail boats, the rough water, the lonely night, the arduous and too often fruitless labor.

We have also fished for cod with the Norwegians and with the Danes, and we have worked with the loin-clad fishermen of

Madras, India, hauling in their seine nets. Out of that experience has come one dominant feeling: respect–not only for the lack of complaint about their grueling profession, but also for the quiet courage of these men who reap the harvest from that dangerous and fickle sea. And respect also for their knowledge of fish.

All fishermen consider fish a day old unfit for a fisherman, but all right for landlubbers–that is, if the landlubbers aren't friends. We have a Norwegian friend, Per Prag, director of the Norwegian National Tourist Office in America, who said, "Tell them if they can't get fresh fish to skip this chapter and go on to poultry, and even then they'd be best off if they buy those birds from a farmer."

Good hard-headed Norwegian advice. But do the best you can. Avoid headless fish; the heads were removed because sunken, dull eyes betray a stale fish. When buying pieces of fish, fillets, or whatever, let your nose do the shopping. Fresh fish do not smell. It is that simple, no matter what the man at the fish market says.

The peasants of the sea aren't fancy with their fresh fish, but they are imaginative. One of our all-time favorites, Whiting *Pizzaiola,* is as uncomplicated as a fish hook. But we find it as poetic as snow on a rose.

BAKED BASS

GREECE

Serves 6

For this "psari plaki" use any white-fleshed ocean, or even river or lake, fish that weighs four pounds after it is scaled and cleaned. We like sea bass and have used black fish and lake trout.

1 fish weighing 4 lb after being cleaned
2½ t salt
½ t pepper
2 T fresh lemon juice
⅓ c olive oil
3 white onions, chopped
2 large, very ripe fresh tomatoes, peeled, seeded, thinly sliced
3 T minced parsley
10 black olives, pitted, cut in half
½ c dry white wine

Sprinkle the fish with half of the salt and pepper and all of the lemon juice. Coat a baking dish with some of the oil and arrange half of the onion and half of the sliced tomatoes on the bottom; sprinkle lightly with salt and pepper. Place the fish on top of the tomatoes; cover it with the remaining onions and tomatoes and the parsley and olives. Spoon the white wine over the top, then the remaining olive oil. Bake, uncovered, in a preheated 375-degree oven for 35 minutes or until the fish flakes with a fork, basting occasionally.

STEWED CALAMARI
(Baby Squid)

ITALY

Serves 6

This is far from being a favored American seafood (except among some Italian-, Spanish-, or Greek-Americans), but if you can drop palate prejudices, you'll discover that this delicate food is, at least, on a par with shrimp. And, again, dropping unfair prejudices, no uglier. For that matter, offhand can you think of anything less appealing to the eye than a lobster? Look where that creature is in popularity. We wonder who first had the courage to eat it.

3 lb baby squid, cleaned (ask the clerk in the fish market to clean them), cut into strips
1½ c red wine vinegar
2 white onions, sliced
½ t salt
¼ t pepper

Place all the ingredients in a bowl. Mix well and marinate for 4 hours.

2 garlic cloves, mashed
4 T olive oil
2 medium-sized white onions, minced
the marinated baby squid (calamari)
3 T of the marinade
2 T minced parsley
2 T tomato paste, blended with 1½ c water
2 c fresh peas, cooked but slightly underdone, or 1 package of frozen peas, defrosted but not cooked
salt and pepper to taste

In a large saucepan brown the garlic in the oil. Discard the garlic. Sauté the onions until they are soft. Drain the *calamari* well. Add the *calamari,* 3 tablespoons of marinade, parsley, and the tomato paste and water to the saucepan. Stir and simmer, covered, for 15 minutes. Stir in the peas; simmer, uncovered, for 10 minutes or until the *calamari* are tender. Taste for seasoning.

TOMATO-CREAMED CODFISH

Serves 6

Baccalà is often stacked like cordwood outside Italian markets and other stores that specialize in ethnic foods. This dried cod has been a food staple of Europe for centuries and in its dry, heavily salted state lasts indefinitely. It doesn't look particularly appetizing, more like something to build a fence with than to eat, but fishermen and country folk (especially the Italians) have devised cooking methods and recipes that make this fish a delicate and appealing dish. The first time we had it we were certain that it would be overwhelmingly "fishy" and strong with salt. We were in for a surprise, and so are you.

2 lb dry cod
1 qt milk
4 T butter
3 T flour
2 c medium cream
2 ripe tomatoes, peeled, seeded, finely chopped
2 egg yolks, beaten
pepper to taste

Soak the cod in cold water for 12 hours, changing the water several times. Rinse well in cold water, dry, and place in a large pot; cover with milk and simmer for 20 minutes or until cod is tender. Drain. Flake the cod. In a saucepan over low heat, melt the butter and slowly blend in the flour to a smooth paste. Stir in the cream, a small amount at a time, blending into a smooth, thick sauce. Add the ripe tomatoes and the flaked cod; simmer for 5 minutes to heat through. In a bowl mix 3 tablespoons of the sauce with the beaten egg yolks; stir back into the sauce. Taste for seasoning. Serve immediately.

FRESH COD AND NOODLES

FRANCE

Serves 6

Cream Sauce

4 T butter
4 T flour
3½ c medium cream
salt and pepper to taste
1 egg yolk, beaten
pinch of nutmeg

In a saucepan over low heat, melt the butter and slowly blend in the flour to a smooth paste. Blend in the cream, a small amount at a time, cooking and stirring to a smooth medium sauce. Season with salt and pepper. Remove from the heat and stir in the egg yolk and nutmeg until well blended.

3 lb fresh cod fillets
1 c milk
1 medium-sized onion, cut in half
leaves from 1 celery rib
salt and pepper to taste
water
½ lb fine noodles, cooked al dente (slightly chewy) in boiling salted water, drained and tossed with 4 T butter
1 c grated Gruyère cheese
3½ c cream sauce (recipe above)
¼ c bread crumbs

In a saucepan place the cod with the milk, onion, celery leaves, salt, pepper, and just enough water to cover. Bring to a boil; then simmer 8 minutes. Remove from the heat and drain. Place the noodles in a well-buttered baking dish; cover with one-half of the cheese and one-third of the sauce. Arrange fillets on top of the sauce. Pour the remaining sauce over the fish, sprinkle with the remaining cheese and bread crumbs, and bake in a preheated 450-degree oven for 15 minutes or until the top is golden.

SWEET AND SOUR FRESH COD

Serves 6

As cod is considered the beef of the sea everywhere in Europe, a number of countries have their own version of this dish.

3 lb fresh cod fillets	**½ c vinegar**
1½ t salt	**2 T white raisins, chopped**
flour for dredging	**1½ T chopped fresh mint**
½ c olive oil	**1½ T pignoli (pine nuts)**
1 c water	**1 T sugar**

Cut cod into serving pieces, sprinkle with salt and dredge lightly with flour. In a deep frying pan heat oil over medium heat and sauté the cod for 8 minutes, browning it on both sides. Pour off the oil. In a saucepan combine the water, vinegar, raisins, mint, pine nuts, and sugar. Blend well and simmer 5 minutes. Pour this sauce over the cod in its pan, cover, and simmer for 3 minutes.

FISH PUDDING

SWEDEN

Serves 6

3½ c water
2½ lb haddock
2 small white onions, thinly sliced
2 small carrots, thinly sliced
1 bay leaf
1½ t salt
½ t pepper
4 T butter
4 T flour
1 c milk
salt and pepper to taste
4 T fine bread crumbs, buttered

In a large shallow pan bring the water to a boil; add the fish, onions, carrots, bay leaf, salt, and pepper. Simmer 12 minutes or until you can flake the haddock with a fork. Remove the fish and flake it. Reduce the liquid in which the fish cooked to one cup. Strain the liquid and set aside. In a saucepan melt the butter and blend in flour to a smooth paste. Over low heat slowly stir in the milk and the reduced liquid that the fish cooked in. Blend into a smooth, thick sauce; season to taste and simmer 2 minutes. Stir in the flaked fish. Butter a casserole; spoon in the fish mixture. Sprinkle the bread crumbs on top and bake, uncovered, in a preheated 375-degree oven for 25 minutes or until crusty brown on top.

SIMPLE FISH SOUFFLÉ

FRANCE

Serves 6

This is a quick but elegant dish that can be easily whipped together with leftover fish. The French use turbot. If you wish, you can use a canned fish–such as red salmon or even tuna, or the more fancy canned crab or lobster–but we prefer moist pieces of leftover cod or flounder.

3 T butter
3 T flour
2 c medium cream
4 egg yolks, beaten
2 c cooked fish, flaked
5 egg whites, beaten
salt and pepper to taste
3 T fine bread crumbs, buttered, mixed with 4 T grated Gruyère cheese

In a saucepan melt the butter; blend in the flour, making a smooth paste. Over low heat slowly stir in the cream, blending into a smooth sauce. Remove from the fire and stir in the beaten egg yolks and the fish. Cool slightly; then fold in the beaten egg whites. Season with salt and pepper. Butter a 2-quart soufflé dish or a casserole. Pour in the fish-egg mixture. Sprinkle the bread crumbs and cheese on top and bake in a preheated 350-degree oven for 30 minutes or until set.

FRIED FLOUNDER WITH PARSLEY SAUCE

DENMARK

Serves 6

This simple but delicious dish we learned from a Danish fisherman who used to have lunch, whenever his ship was in, at the Terminus Hotel in Copenhagen, a small but elegant place known to very few tourists. To the annoyance of the chef, he took us into the kitchen there and showed us how to cook this dish. The Danes use *plaice,* a firm-fleshed fish from the cold waters of the North Sea, which is the same as the famed Dover sole, in our view. You need any sole or flounder you can get. But it must be fresh or forget it.

Our fisherman friend liked parsley sauce with this. Make it first so the cooked fish won't have to wait.

Parsley Sauce

3 T butter
2 T flour
1 c chicken broth
3 T minced parsley
1 T lemon juice
salt to taste

In a saucepan melt the butter; gradually blend in the flour to a smooth paste. Over low heat slowly stir in the chicken broth, blending into a smooth, thickish sauce. Simmer for 5 minutes. Stir in the parsley, then the lemon juice. Off the heat stir in salt to your taste. Spoon this over the cooked fish fillets.

Cooking the Fillets

6 fillets of flounder, weighing ½ lb each	**3 eggs, beaten**
salt to taste	**about 1 c bread crumbs**
flour for dredging	**4 T butter**
	2 T olive oil

Sprinkle the fillets lightly with salt; dredge them with flour. Dip the fillets in the beaten egg, then into the bread crumbs. In a frying pan heat the butter and oil. Cook the fish over medium heat 3 minutes on each side until golden. The point with these fragile-textured fish is not to overcook. They should flake with a fork but be moist inside.

FROG LEGS PROVENÇALE

FRANCE

Serves 6

The French countryman (or his wife) is so skillful in the kitchen with the frogs that he (or she) catches at night in nearby ponds and swampy areas that this recipe has become internationally famous. Those of you who do not know how delicious the delicate white meat of the frog's hind legs can be are in for a treat. If you can't catch your own, frog legs are for sale frozen in many markets.

18 pairs frog legs	**1½ sticks butter (¾ c)**
1 qt milk	**4 garlic cloves, minced**
5 T flour	**juice of 2 lemons**
2 t salt	**½ c minced parsley**
1 t pepper	**salt and pepper to taste**
¼ c olive oil (add more if necessary)	**lemon wedges for garnish**

Soak the frog legs in milk in the refrigerator for 4 hours. Dry on paper towels. Place the flour, the 2 teaspoons of salt, the teaspoon of pepper, and the frog legs in a clean paper bag; shake well, until each pair is lightly coated. In a saucepan heat the olive oil and sauté the frog legs, a few at a time (do not crowd), until they are lightly browned on both sides and crispy. Do not overcook; they should be moist. Keep the frog legs warm. In another saucepan melt the butter; sauté the garlic until it is soft and the butter is slightly brown. Stir in the lemon juice, parsley, salt, and pepper. Pour this sauce over the frog legs and serve immediately with the lemon wedges.

HALIBUT WITH TOMATOES

CHINA

Serves 6

- **1 T salt**
- **3 1-lb halibut fillets**
- **2 T fermented black beans, well washed, drained, minced**
- **1 large garlic clove, minced**
- **3 scallions (white part only), minced**
- **3 very thin slices ginger root, minced**
- **2½ T rice wine (if you can't get it, use dry white wine)**
- **2 T soy sauce**
- **1 t salt**
- **1 t sugar**
- **3 ripe tomatoes, peeled, seeded, chopped**

Sprinkle the tablespoon of salt on both sides of the fillets; let stand ½ hour. Wipe off the salt and place the fish in a single layer in a shallow pot. In a bowl combine the beans, garlic, scallions, ginger root, wine, soy sauce, salt, sugar, and tomatoes. Mix well and spoon over the fillets. Cover the pot tightly and simmer for 25 minutes or until the fish flakes with a fork.

PAELLA

SPAIN

Serves 8

Paella is a peasant specialty, with country folk in Spain having it often and farm hands even cooking the rice concoction in the fields. It also is the national dish of Spain, served in most restaurants in several versions. It can be offered with just game or fish, and we have had it with only sausage and shellfish, but the paella said to be most appreciated is this one we learned from the chef at Botin, probably Spain's oldest restaurant and Madrid's most popular. When the paella is served in the round metal pan in which it is cooked, it appears to be a complicated dish with several kinds of meat, fish, and vegetables. That look is deceptive. Most items are cooked separately and then assembled and simmered with the rice before serving. So don't let the list of ingredients put you off. This is a dish with something for everyone. It's not difficult to prepare, and once you master it, your name could become a household word among your friends and neighbors.

The large circular paella pan, the *paellera,* is perfect, but if you haven't got one, a very large shallow pan that can go from the top of the stove into the oven will do. As you can see from the list of ingredients, the pan must not be too shallow.

1 3-lb chicken, cut up (do not use back or wing tips)—breast cut into 4 pieces, thighs into 2 pieces
salt and pepper to taste
½ c olive oil
8 pieces fresh haddock, each large enough for a small serving
1 large yellow onion, chopped
1 large garlic clove, minced
1 c raw lean pork, diced
1 large ripe fresh tomato (or one cup of canned), peeled, seeded, and chopped
3 c long-grained, uncooked rice
½ t powdered saffron
7 c chicken broth
½ c fresh green peas, undercooked in salted water, or defrosted frozen ones

½ c fresh green string beans, cut up, undercooked in salted water, or defrosted frozen ones
6 chorizos (Spanish sausages) or sweet Italian sausages, skins pricked in several places, simmered in water 10 minutes, drained, sautéed in oil until evenly browned, and cut into ¼-inch-thick slices
16 small fresh shrimps, shells removed and deveined
16 clams or mussels, or both, scrubbed clean
8 thin strips pimiento
1 package frozen artichoke hearts, cooked according to directions on package

Season the chicken pieces with salt and pepper. Heat one-half of the oil in a paella pan and evenly brown the chicken. Remove the chicken and set aside. Pour more oil in pan if necessary; season and sauté the haddock 2 minutes on each side. Remove and set aside. Add the onions, garlic, and pork; season and sauté for 10 minutes or until the pork is browned. Stir in the tomato, rice, saffron, and 6 cups of chicken broth. Simmer for 10 minutes. Sprinkle peas and string beans over the rice. Arrange the chicken, haddock, sausage slices, shrimps, and clams (or mussels) on top of the rice, pushing the pieces gently down into the rice. Bring to a simmer on top of the stove; then place, uncovered, in a preheated 350-degree oven for 15 minutes or until the rice has absorbed all of the broth. Test to see if the rice is tender (yet not too soft). If not, add a small amount of hot chicken broth and return pan to the oven until the rice is tender. Garnish with the pimiento strips and artichoke hearts and return to the oven for 5 minutes. Let the paella stand for a few minutes and serve right from the pan.

HERRING CUSTARD

NORWAY

Serves 6

2 salt herring (each weighing about 1¼ lb)
6 medium-sized potatoes, thinly sliced
black pepper to taste
4 medium-sized white onions, thinly sliced
3 eggs beaten with 2 c milk

Soak the salt herring in cold water for 12 hours, changing the water several times. Drain them; cut off heads and tails; remove skin and bones and cut the herring into ½-inch-thick slices. Butter a baking dish and place a layer of potatoes on the bottom (sprinkling each layer of potatoes with pepper), then a layer of herring, then one of onions, and so on, ending with potatoes. Pour the egg-milk mixture over the layers. Bake, uncovered, in a preheated 375-degree oven for 40 minutes or until the custard is set and the potatoes are cooked.

JUTLAND FISHERMAN'S PIE

DENMARK

Serves 6

3 lb fresh cod fillets
salt and pepper to taste
8 T butter
1 medium-sized white onion, minced
5 c mashed potatoes—seasoned with salt, pepper, and cream
½ c grated Havarti cheese (or a cheese of your choice)
¼ c bread crumbs

Sprinkle the fillets with salt and pepper on both sides. In a frying pan melt 4 tablespoons of the butter and sauté fillets until they are golden on both sides, but still slightly underdone inside (about 4 minutes on each side). Place the fillets in one layer in a well-buttered baking dish. Sauté the onions in 2 tablespoons of butter until they are soft. Scatter the onions over the fillets. Arrange a layer of the potatoes to cover the fillets. Sprinkle with the cheese, then the bread crumbs, and dot with the remaining butter. Bake, uncovered, in a preheated 350-degree oven for 25 minutes or until the top is golden.

LUBINA
(Sea Bass)

SPAIN

Serves 6

2 sticks (1 c) butter, softened
3 T dry white wine
1 t salt
½ t pepper
juice of 1 lemon
1 4-lb sea bass (head and tail saved after cleaning)

In a bowl mix into a paste the soft butter, wine, salt, pepper, and lemon juice. Place the bass in a buttered baking dish just large enough to hold it. Coat the fish with the butter paste. Bake it in a preheated 350-degree oven, uncovered, for 45 minutes or until you can flake it with a fork, basting it several times with the liquid in the pan. While the bass is cooking, prepare the sauce.

Sauce

2 small white onions, chopped
2 T butter
1 T olive oil
2 large ripe tomatoes, peeled, seeded, chopped
1 c dry white wine
1 c water
1 small bay leaf
salt and pepper to taste
the bass head and tail
2 T flour
½ lb small shrimp, shelled, deveined
2 T chopped parsley

In a saucepan sauté the onions in the hot butter and the oil until soft. Stir in the tomatoes, wine, water, bay leaf, salt, and pepper. Add the bass head and tail. Cover the pan and simmer for 25 minutes. Make a smooth paste of the flour and some of the liquid in the saucepan; stir into the sauce and simmer, uncovered, until the sauce thickens. Discard the bass head and tail and the bay leaf. Add the shrimp to the sauce and simmer 2 minutes. Serve the bass whole on a hot platter, with the shrimp lined down the center. Sprinkle the parsley over the shrimp and pass the sauce at the table.

MUSSELS WITH SCALLIONS AND RICE

GREECE

Serves 6

You might say that eaters and cookers of mussels have fallen into a rut. Almost any French menu you read features *Moules Marinière* as do the majority of cookbooks. We know dozens of people who believe that they can't be cooked any other way. But mussels are mostly unappreciated in this country, losing out to clams and shrimps. In our opinion they are superior to clams—more delicate, with a softer, more persuasive personality.

8 young scallions (white and green parts), chopped
2 garlic cloves, minced
½ c olive oil
2 T tomato paste
1½ c dry white wine
4 doz mussels, well scrubbed
1½ c boiling water
1½ t salt
1 c uncooked rice
1 c currants

In a large deep saucepan sauté the scallions and garlic in the oil until soft. Stir in the tomato paste and wine; add the mussels. Cover the pan tightly and simmer for 10 minutes or just until the mussels have opened their shells, discarding any that are unopened. Pour in the boiling water; add the salt, rice, and currants; stir well. Cover and simmer for about 15 minutes or until the rice is cooked. Rice should be *al dente*—slightly chewy, not soft. Taste for seasoning. Serve the mussels in their shells on a bed of rice and currants.

SOLE IN SOUR CREAM

POLAND

Serves 6

This recipe for *Sola Zapiekana* was taught us by a Polish neighbor who learned it from his mother in Warsaw. He said that they also cooked perch and trout this way. It's unique.

6 fillets of sole or flounder, each weighing ½ lb
salt to taste
flour for dredging
5 T butter
1 T olive oil
¼ c grated Parmesan cheese
½ t flour
1 c sour cream
½ c buttered bread crumbs

Season the fillets with salt and dredge them with flour. In a frying pan heat the butter and oil and lightly brown the fish on both sides. Place the fish in a buttered, shallow baking dish. Sprinkle the cheese over the fish. Mix the ½ teaspoon of flour with the sour cream and spoon it over the fish. Sprinkle the bread crumbs on top and bake, uncovered, in a preheated 375-degree oven for 15 minutes or until the fish flakes with a fork and the bread crumbs are crusty brown.

FRANK GAGLIARDI'S STEAMED WHITING WITH CLAMS

ITALY

Serves 6

Frank Gagliardi, who introduced us to this recipe, is one of those lucky naturals–a born cook. He specializes in the so-called peasant style, which, as we have said often, simply means uncomplicated and superb. Frank has learned many recipes from his Italian family, but he is also a creator and has come up with unique specialties of his own. We suspect that this is one. He has a magic touch with fish.

6 whiting, weighing ½ lb each after being cleaned
4 T olive oil
salt and pepper to taste
2 garlic cloves, minced, mixed with 3 T minced parsley
6 T fresh lemon juice
2 to 3 c dry white wine
24 clams, well scrubbed

Coat the fish with the oil and place them, skin side down, side by side in a shallow ovenproof pot. Salt and pepper the fish and distribute the garlic-parsley mixture over them; sprinkle with lemon juice; then pour wine around the fish to the depth of ½ inch. Cover; heat on top of the stove to a simmer. Then cook in a preheated 350-degree oven for 20 minutes. Add clams, return to the oven, uncovered, and cook 10 minutes more or until fish flakes with a fork and clams open. Serve in large bowls with the broth. Pass crusty, buttered bread and chilled white wine.

FRANK GAGLIARDI'S WHITING PIZZAIOLA

ITALY

Serves 6

6 whiting, weighing ½ lb each after being cleaned
salt and pepper
1 (1-lb, 12-oz) can of tomatoes, mashed into small pieces
2 garlic cloves, minced
2 T olive oil
4 t raisins, chopped
½ t dry basil
¼ t dry oregano
1 c water
3 T bread crumbs

In a shallow ovenproof pot place the fish, skin side down. Sprinkle lightly with salt and pepper. In a saucepan combine the tomatoes, garlic, olive oil, raisins, basil, oregano, and salt and pepper to taste. Stir in the water, bring to a boil; then simmer, uncovered, for 20 minutes, stirring often. Spoon the tomato sauce over the fish, sprinkle with the bread crumbs, and bake in a preheated 350-degree oven for 30 minutes or until the fish flakes with a fork.

CHAPTER FIVE

Poultry and Rabbit

If you cook chicken like a peasant, you'll eat like Emperor Napoleon.

History records that Napoleon had a difficult time defeating the Austrian army near Marengo, in the mountainous region of Italy's Piedmont. After the battle, while resting under a tree beside the Bormida River, Napoleon told his aide that he was tired of the food prepared by the catering corps and asked him to supply something more interesting, as it was a night to celebrate.

The aide found a peasant woman in Marengo who offered her services. She prepared chicken in the style of her region, a dish that had been cooked at fiestas for generations. As served to Napoleon, it was a colorful offering with the chicken surrounded by shrimps and deep-fried eggs and fried bread. Napoleon was so impressed with the dish that he introduced it (and the eggs) into the French cuisine, never mentioning that they were created by an Italian peasant. Of Corsican peasant stock himself, the self-proclaimed emperor took great pains to keep every aspect of his life on the highest level, even if it meant being dishonest to himself and others.

Not so our mentor Antoine Gilly, who always gave credit where it was due. When he was chef on the famed Blue Train that ran between Paris and the Riviera, his deep-fried eggs were a great success. On the menu M. Gilly stated that the "French fried Eggs" were first served Napoleon at Marengo by an Italian peasant woman. Try the eggs. They are broken into a dish and carefully slid into 2 cups of oil heated to 400 degrees, cooked 3 minutes, and turned often so they are evenly browned.

On the subject of that famed chef, Antoine Gilly is a devotee (as are many who respect fine food) of that superb peasant-farmer-hunter's favorite, rabbit. We include a rabbit recipe of M. Gilly here, and we also quote him on the subject.

"It is too bad," he says, "that so many Americans are squeamish about rabbit. Not only is its white meat delicious, but also a rabbit has little fat, thus is very low in cholesterol. It has its own distinctly delicate flavor gained from eating only clean, natural, organic foods, such as grasses and other vegetation. In fact, the rabbit diet is not unlike that of beef cattle. But in my opinion the flesh of the rabbit is superior."

A king, a prince, two prime ministers, various noblemen, several maharajas, and hundreds of other greats and near-greats listened when Antoine Gilly commented on food. Perhaps you should too. (But if you still have qualms, use chicken.)

Domestic rabbit meat is available frozen in many markets. It has become more expensive than chicken, but we feel it is worth the price. Other peasant specialties are squabs, pigeons, doves, quail, pheasant, guinea hen, and partridge, but since they are difficult to obtain, we have excluded them here.

BALKAN BUTTERY ROAST CHICKEN

Serves 6

Most country folk know the infinite uses of butter well, and, in many places (hard to believe!) still produce it on their farms. There is no more successful wedding of butter and chicken than in the following dish, sometimes served for a Balkan Sunday dinner.

1 5-lb roasting chicken
1 stick (8 T) butter
salt and pepper
4 sprigs parsley
4 garlic cloves
3 T olive oil

Divide butter in half. Rub the inside of the chicken with half of the butter and leave whatever is left of the half-stick inside the bird. Sprinkle the inside of the bird with salt and pepper; then place the parsley and 2 garlic cloves inside the bird. Truss the chicken. Generously rub the outside with the rest of the butter and sprinkle it with salt. Place the chicken, the remaining garlic, and olive oil in a roasting pan and bake, uncovered, in a preheated 375-degree oven (basting the bird with the pan juices every 15 minutes) for 1½ hours or until the chicken is fork-tender. It should emerge from the oven golden brown and juicy.

CARIBBEAN RICE WITH CHICKEN

Serves 6

1 4-lb chicken, cut up (cut the breasts into 3 pieces, the thighs into 2 pieces)
1½ T salt
4 peppercorns
½ t dry oregano
1 large garlic clove, quartered
2 T olive oil
2 t vinegar
3 T lard (or oil)
¼ lb ham, finely diced
¼ lb salt pork, finely diced
2 medium-sized onions, finely chopped
1 large green pepper, seeds and white part removed, chopped
1 sweet chili pepper, seeds and white part removed, chopped
2 sprigs cilantro (coriander) or parsley
8 green olives, pitted and coarsely chopped
1 t capers, rinsed, drained, and finely chopped
2 large tomatoes, peeled, seeded, and chopped
2½ c uncooked rice, washed and drained
2 c boiling chicken broth
2 c boiling water
1 package frozen small green peas, defrosted but not cooked
2 pimientos, cut into strips and warmed just before serving

Dry the chicken pieces well with paper towels. With a mortar and pestle mash together the salt, peppercorns, oregano, garlic, olive oil, and vinegar. Rub the chicken pieces with this mixture. In a large ovenproof casserole heat 1 tablespoon of lard (or oil) over medium heat. Brown the ham and salt pork dices. Remove them with a slotted spoon; set aside. Add the chicken to the pot and brown it evenly. Remove the chicken. Add the chopped onions, green pepper, sweet chili pepper, and the *cilantro* (if you are using parsley, add it later) to the pot. Sauté until the onions are soft but not brown. Add the green olives, capers, and tomatoes and simmer for 10 minutes or until most of the liquid from the tomatoes has cooked off. Return the ham, salt pork, and chicken to the pot. Stir in the rice, boiling broth, water, and the remaining 2 tablespoons of lard (or oil). Mix well but carefully. Bring to a boil on top of the stove, cover pot, and bake in a preheated 350-degree oven for 20 minutes, fluffing the rice with a fork after 15 minutes. Add the peas (and parsley if used) and return to the oven for 10 minutes or until the chicken is tender and the liquid has been absorbed. Garnish the rice with the pimientos and serve from the pot.

CHICKEN WITH 30 CLOVES OF GARLIC

BASQUE PROVINCES

Serves 6

2 3-lb chickens, cut up
30 garlic cloves, peeled, left whole
½ c olive oil
½ c white vermouth
3 leeks, white part only, thinly sliced
8 sprigs parsley
2 t salt
1 t dry tarragon
½ t pepper
pinch of dry rosemary

Place the chicken pieces and garlic in a large casserole. Pour in the oil and vermouth. Toss the chicken pieces in the oil and vermouth. Add the leeks, parsley, salt, tarragon, pepper, and rosemary. Mix everything well with your hands. Cover the casserole snugly with aluminum foil. Place the top of the pan over the foil, wrap with another piece of foil, and seal around the edge of the lid with masking tape. Place in a preheated 375-degree oven for 1 hour. The dramatic way to serve the dish is to unmask it at the table so the aroma can come wafting out. Crusty warm bread, spread with the garlic that cooked with the chicken, is served with this. Surprisingly, the garlic is sweet and delicious and the chicken is just nicely scented with it, not overwhelmed.

MARIA CIFELLI LIMONCELLI'S CHICKEN CACCIATORE

ITALY

Serves 6

2 3-lb chickens, cut up
salt and pepper
5 T olive oil
1 medium-sized onion, chopped
1 garlic clove, minced
1 medium-sized celery rib, scraped, chopped
1 bay leaf
pinch of oregano
1½ c dry white wine

Season the chicken pieces with salt and pepper. In a frying pan brown the chicken pieces evenly in the olive oil. As they brown, transfer them to a warm dish. After all the chicken has been browned, pour off all but about 2 tablespoons of the fat. Stir in the onion, garlic, and celery and sauté until they are soft. Add the bay leaf, oregano, and dry white wine and stir, scraping the bottom of the pan. Return the chicken pieces to the pan, cover, and simmer for 35 minutes or until the chicken is fork tender. If the liquid cooks off, add a small amount of hot water to the pan. Sometimes Maria varied this by adding a small can of tomatoes and red, instead of white, wine.

PALMINA THOMPSON'S CHICKEN BREASTS AND MUSHROOMS

Serves 6

6 T butter
6 medium-sized, fresh mushrooms, thinly sliced
3 T flour
1 c chicken broth
½ c dry white wine
1 c sour cream
salt and pepper to taste
3 large whole chicken breasts, split, not boned, skin removed

In a saucepan heat 2 tablespoons of the butter and sauté the mushrooms 3 minutes. Remove the mushrooms and put aside. In the same saucepan melt the remaining butter and over low heat slowly blend in the flour to a smooth paste. Slowly pour in the chicken broth, stirring to a smooth, thickened sauce. Simmer 5 minutes. Pour in the wine and sour cream; gently simmer, uncovered, 5 minutes, stirring constantly. Do not boil. Taste for seasoning. Stir the reserved mushrooms into the sauce. Place the chicken breasts in a large casserole. Pour the mushroom sauce over them. Cook, uncovered, in a preheated 350-degree oven for 45 minutes or until the chicken breasts are fork tender. Serve with fine noodles.

CHINESE CHICKEN BREASTS

CANTON

Serves 6

5 T soy sauce
2 t sugar
2 T white wine
2 T cornstarch
3 whole, boned chicken breasts, cut into large dices
2 T peanut oil
1 c bean sprouts
1 c snow peas
½ c bamboo shoots, shredded
3 T sherry

In a large bowl combine 3 tablespoons of the soy sauce, 1 teaspoon of the sugar, the white wine, and cornstarch. Blend well. Marinate the chicken in this for 2 hours, stirring from time to time. Heat the peanut oil in a wok or frying pan and stir-fry the chicken dices for 4 minutes. Add the bean sprouts, snow peas, bamboo shoots, the remaining soy sauce, sugar, and the sherry to the chicken. Stir-fry for about 2 minutes or until the chicken is fork tender, but the vegetables are still crisp. Serve with Pork Fried Rice.

CHICKEN WITH ONIONS

GREECE

Serves 6

½ c flour
1 T salt
1 t pepper
2 3-lb chickens, cut up
4 T olive oil
10 small white onions, chopped
3 garlic cloves, minced
2 c chicken broth, heated

Combine the flour, salt, and pepper in a clean paper bag. Add the chicken pieces and shake them until they are all evenly coated with the flour. In a frying pan heat the oil and brown the chicken evenly. Transfer the chicken to a baking dish. Stir the onions and garlic into the same frying pan, adding more oil if necessary. Sauté until the onions are soft. Add the heated chicken broth; stir, loosening particles on bottom of pan, and simmer until the onion sauce is smooth and golden. Taste for seasoning. Pour this sauce over the chicken pieces, cover, and cook in a preheated 350-degree oven for 30 minutes or until the chicken is fork tender. Rabbit can be used instead of chicken.

MADELINE ALTMAN'S CHICKEN RISO

Serves 6

Madeline Altman, the eldest daughter of Maria Cifelli Limoncelli and Pasquale Limoncelli, has inherited her mother's cooking talent and is a creator—often inventing her own recipes, nearly always with an Italian touch. Commensurate with her training, she is restrained and tasteful with her portions and makes all ingredients count. The result is delicious, delicately cooked food that always has guests asking for more.

flour for dredging (about 1 c)
1½ T salt
½ t dry oregano
2 3-lb chickens, cut up
9 T butter
2 T olive oil
4 T flour for the sauce
2 c chicken broth
½ c medium cream
juice of ½ lemon
salt and pepper to taste
2 small white onions, finely minced
2 T chopped, broad-leafed Italian parsley
⅛ t dry thyme
2 c cooked rice, slightly underdone

Blend the flour with the salt and oregano; dredge the chicken pieces with the seasoned flour. In a saucepan heat 4 tablespoons of the butter and the olive oil. Brown the chicken evenly; remove it and set aside. Discard the fat in the pan. Melt the remaining butter in the same saucepan; slowly blend in the 4 tablespoons of flour to a smooth paste. Over low heat slowly stir in the chicken broth, a small amount at a time, stirring into a smooth, medium sauce. Stir in the cream and the lemon juice. Simmer 3 minutes. Taste for seasoning. Stir in the onions, parsley, and thyme. Simmer, stirring, 3 minutes. Place the cooked rice in a large casserole. Pour ½ of the cream sauce over the rice. Arrange the browned chicken pieces on top; pour the remaining sauce over. Cover the casserole and bake in a preheated 375-degree oven for 25 minutes or until the chicken is fork tender.

CHICKEN ROMANO

ITALY

Serves 6

6 half chicken breasts (not boned)
6 chicken thighs
6 T olive oil
2 garlic cloves, peeled, cut into halves
5 T chopped, broad-leafed Italian parsley
1½ t salt
½ t pepper
1½ c bread crumbs
2 t paprika
6 medium-sized potatoes, quartered

In a large bowl place the chicken parts, oil, garlic, parsley, salt, and pepper. Toss well together; place in the refrigerator and marinate for 4 hours. Remove the chicken pieces from marinade and dredge with bread crumbs. Save the marinade in the bowl. In a large baking dish arrange the chicken; sprinkle with paprika. Place the potato quarters in the bowl in which the chicken marinated; toss well, coating them with the remaining oil and parsley. Arrange potatoes between the chicken pieces. Place the baking dish, uncovered, in a preheated 400-degree oven and cook for 20 minutes. Turn the potatoes so they will brown evenly. Return to the oven and cook for 20 minutes. This dish can have a taste variation by using 1 teaspoon of dry oregano and 3 tablespoons of chopped parsley.

CHICKEN TANDOORI

INDIA

Serves 6

This is famous in India—almost its national dish. Classically, it is cooked in a *tandoor*, which is a four-foot cylindrical clay oven usually buried in the ground. Wood is the fuel, or sometimes charcoal. When the fire is banked and the coals glowing, the heat in the oven becomes concentrated and intense. The oven narrows toward the top into an opening about a foot wide. Food, especially chicken and various kabobs, is placed on oiled skewers and quickly cooked. The results are extremely flavorsome and juicy. We have simplified and adapted this recipe so you can use broiler chickens in your own oven.

3 broilers, split in half and skinned
1 qt natural plain yogurt
¼ c fresh lemon or lime juice
3 T olive oil
3 large garlic cloves, crushed
1½ T curry powder
¼ t ground ginger
¼ t ground cumin
¼ t coriander

Cut small slits in the chicken halves. Place in a large bowl. Combine the yogurt, lemon or lime juice, olive oil, garlic, curry powder, ginger, cumin, and coriander and mix well. Pour this mixture over the chicken halves and marinate at least 3 hours in the refrigerator. Remove the chicken at least 1 hour before cooking. Discard garlic. Broil slowly, basting with the marinade, for 25 to 30 minutes on each side until chicken is tender.

COQ AU VIN ANTOINE GILLY

FRANCE

Serves 6

½ lb salt pork, diced, blanched 2 minutes, drained, rinsed under cold water, and dried
2 3-lb chickens, cut up
salt and pepper
flour for dredging
4 T butter
3 oz cognac, slightly warmed
18 small white onions
18 medium-sized, white mushroom caps
3 c dry red wine
2 c chicken broth
bouquet garni (1 bay leaf, 3 sprigs parsley, pinch of thyme tied in a cheesecloth)
1 garlic clove, chopped
2 T chopped parsley

In a saucepan sauté the salt pork for 3 minutes; remove the salt pork and reserve it and the fat. Salt and pepper the chicken pieces; dredge them with flour and gently shake off any excess flour. Add the butter to the pan with the salt pork fat and when hot add the chicken pieces. Sauté, turning the pieces, until golden. Transfer to a casserole. Pour the cognac over the chicken; ignite it and baste the chicken until the flame dies out. In the pan the chicken sautéed in, sauté the onions until golden, adding more butter if necessary. Transfer to the chicken casserole. Sauté the mushrooms in the same pan for 1 minute. Remove and reserve. Place the salt pork in the same pan, cover, and simmer for 10 minutes. Transfer the salt pork to the chicken casserole. Pour off the excess fat from the pan the salt pork simmered in. Pour in the wine and broth; add bouquet garni and the garlic. Simmer for 5 minutes, scraping the bottom of the pan. Pour the wine-broth mixture into the chicken casserole, cover, and cook in a preheated 325-degree oven for 30 minutes. Add the mushrooms and continue to cook, covered, another ½ hour or until chicken is tender. Remove bouquet garni. Taste for seasoning. Sprinkle with chopped parsley and serve from the casserole.

CORNISH GAME HENS WITH WINEKRAUT

ALSACE-LORRAINE

Serves 6

In Europe, partridge, pheasant, or guinea hen are used, but Cornish hens are an excellent substitute.

3 T butter
2 T olive oil
3 Cornish game hens, large enough for ½ bird per serving
salt and pepper
4 small white onions, chopped
2 garlic cloves, chopped
1 qt sauerkraut, drained
1½ t caraway seeds
1 pt (2 c) dry white wine

In a deep casserole heat the butter and oil. Season the game hens with salt and pepper. Brown the birds evenly. Remove and set aside. Add the onions and garlic to the pot and sauté until they are soft but not brown. Stir in the sauerkraut; sprinkle with caraway seeds and blend well. Simmer the sauerkraut 15 minutes. Pour in the white wine. Toss the sauerkraut, mixing it well with the wine. Add the game hens; cover them with the sauerkraut. Cover the pot. Place in a preheated 350-degree oven for one hour or until the game hens are fork tender.

MOLE POBLANO

MEXICO

Serves 6

- **3 whole (6 halves) chicken breasts**
- **6 chicken thighs**
- **1 medium-sized onion, left whole**
- **1 celery rib**
- **1 carrot**
- **2 t salt**
- **3 c chicken broth (use liquid the chicken cooked in)**
- **½ c almonds, toasted, coarsely chopped**
- **1 T sesame seeds, toasted**
- **½ t aniseed**
- **1 tortilla or 1 slice toasted stale bread**
- **½ c seedless raisins**
- **½ square bitter chocolate, grated**
- **4 t red chili powder**
- **½ t powdered cinnamon**
- **⅛ t ground cloves**
- **2 T lard (or oil)**
- **2 medium-sized onions, chopped**
- **2 garlic cloves, chopped**
- **2 T flour**
- **½ c tomato puree**
- **chopped cilantro (coriander) or parsley**

Place the chicken pieces in a pot with the whole onion, celery, carrot, and 1 teaspoon of salt. Cover with water; bring to a boil, cover, and simmer for 20 minutes or until the chicken pieces are almost tender (do not overcook; they will cook more later). In a blender combine 1 cup of the chicken stock (strained), the almonds, sesame seeds, aniseeds, the tortilla (or bread), raisins, chocolate, chili powder, cinnamon, and cloves and blend to a smooth puree. In a large pot, over medium heat, melt the lard; add the chopped onions and garlic and sauté until the onions are soft. Lower the heat and blend in the flour to a smooth golden paste. Add the ingredients from the blender. Simmer, stirring constantly, until well mixed and smooth, about 2 minutes; stir in the tomato puree and mix well. Stir in 1 cup of the chicken stock and the remaining teaspoon of salt. Simmer about 10 minutes until the sauce begins to thicken. Add the chicken pieces; spoon the sauce over them and simmer, uncovered, about 20 minutes or until the chicken is fork tender and the sauce is thick. If the sauce becomes too thick (it should be quite thick, however), add small amounts of hot broth. Taste for seasoning. Sprinkle with the *cilantro* or parsley.

CHICKEN WITH BLACK OLIVES AND ANCHOVIES

ITALY

Serves 6

We enjoyed this dish in a village outside of Bologna. We ordered it because a large table crowded with people of the village were obviously enjoying it. It has become a favorite.

2 3-lb chickens, cut up
salt and pepper
3 T butter
2 T olive oil
2 small onions, minced
1 large garlic clove, minced
1 c dry white wine
juice of 1 lemon
2 c chicken broth
½ t dry oregano
3 T sliced Italian black olives
8 anchovies, rinsed in cold water and dried, cut up

Season the chicken pieces with salt and pepper. In a deep frying pan brown the chicken evenly in the butter and oil, adding more oil if necessary. Remove the chicken and set aside. If fat remains in the pan, pour off all but 1 tablespoon (if there is no fat, add 1 tablespoon of olive oil). Stir in the onions and garlic; cook over medium heat, stirring until soft and slightly golden. Add the wine and lemon juice and simmer, uncovered, scraping the bottom of the pan, until the liquid has reduced by half. Add the chicken broth and bring to a boil; lower the heat and add the oregano and the browned chicken. Cover the pan and simmer for

25 minutes or until the chicken is fork tender. Transfer the chicken to a hot serving dish and keep warm. Add the black olives and anchovies and simmer, uncovered, over medium heat, stirring, for 5 minutes. Taste for seasoning. Spoon this sauce over the chicken and serve.

CHICKEN MARENGO

ITALY

Serves 6

flour for dredging (about 1 c)
1½ t salt
½ t pepper
⅛ t ground allspice
2 3-lb chickens, cut up
4 T butter
2 T olive oil
18 small white onions
2 garlic cloves, minced
1 c dry white wine
1½ oz brandy
2 large tomatoes, peeled, seeded, chopped (or 2 c of canned)
12 small whole mushrooms, sautéed 2 minutes in 2 T of butter
8 pitted black olives
2 T chopped parsley

Mix together the flour, salt, pepper, and allspice. Dredge the chicken pieces with this mixture. In a large frying pan brown the chicken pieces evenly in the butter and oil. Transfer the chicken to a casserole. Add the onions, garlic, wine, brandy, and tomatoes to the casserole; cover and place in a preheated 350-degree oven for 30 minutes or until the chicken is fork tender. Stir in the mushrooms and olives and cook for 10 minutes. Sprinkle with parsley before serving.

DUCK BRAISED IN RED WINE AND RED CABBAGE

POLAND

Serves 6

2 4-lb ducklings
4 T butter
salt and pepper
1 2-inch cube of fatback, blanched in hot water, drained, cut into small dices
1 medium-sized yellow onion, chopped
1 garlic clove, minced
1 solid, medium-sized head red cabbage, shredded, blanched in salted water, and well drained (do not use the core)
1 c dry red wine
2 t sugar
2 t caraway seeds
2 T of drippings from the duck roasting pan

Dry the ducks with paper towels. Rub them with the butter; then sprinkle them with salt and pepper. Place the ducks in a roasting pan and then into a preheated 450-degree oven, uncovered, for 30 minutes or until nicely browned all over (turn the ducks to brown them evenly). In a casserole sauté the small dices of fatback until they are golden. Pour off all but about 2 tablespoons of fat; add the onions and garlic and sauté until they are soft. Stir the cabbage, red wine, sugar, and caraway seeds into the casserole. Sprinkle with salt and pepper; cover and simmer 10 minutes. Stir in 2 tablespoons of the fat drippings from the roasting pan. Transfer the ducks to the pot with the cabbage, spooning some of the cabbage over them. Cover the pot, turn the oven down to 350 degrees, and cook about 1 hour or until the ducks and cabbage are tender. If midway in the cooking the liquid cooks off, add a small amount of warm red wine.

DUCKS POACHED IN BEER

GERMANY

Serves 6

Ducks look fat and one seems ample to serve four, but looks are deceptive. Two are just about right for six. There isn't much meat on the wings, and the breast meat is not as thick as it is on most other fowl.

2 4-lb ducks, cut up
1½ t salt
½ t dry tarragon
flour for dredging
5 T butter
1 T olive oil
1 c beer
1 c beef broth
2 garlic cloves
1 white onion
1 small bay leaf
1 small strip orange rind
1 carrot
¼ t dry marjoram
2 T arrowroot, blended with 3 T of water

Sprinkle the duck with salt and tarragon and dredge it with flour. In a deep saucepan melt the butter and oil and brown the duck pieces evenly. Pour off the fat. Pour in the beer and beef broth and bring to a simmer; then add the garlic, onion, bay leaf, orange rind, carrot, and marjoram. Cover the pan and simmer for 45 minutes or until the duck pieces are fork-tender. Transfer the duck pieces to a hot serving dish. Spoon the grease from the surface of the sauce, stir in the arrowroot blended with water, bring to a simmer, and stir until the sauce is smooth and thickened. Serve immediately (arrowroot does not hold very long) and pass the sauce at the table.

ROAST GOOSE

AUSTRIA

Serves 6

Too few of us realize how delicious geese are. While we serve turkey for most holiday occasions, the Europeans offer roast goose, usually one from the barnyard. Geese for roasting should not weigh more than 10 pounds. The heavier birds tend to be tough. A goose does not have the flesh that a turkey of equal size has, and although a 10-pound goose will serve 6, the servings cannot be lavish. The flesh is dark and moist and full of flavor. They are fatty birds and must be given special treatment.

1 10-lb goose
1 lemon, cut in half
1 T dry white wine
salt and pepper
3 T butter
1 T olive oil
2 small tart green apples, peeled, cored, diced
3 small white onions, minced
1 lb sauerkraut, drained
1 T caraway seeds
½ c dry white wine
2 small potatoes, grated
1½ c boiling water

Remove all of the yellow globs of fat from inside the goose; then rub the cavity with the lemon halves. Sprinkle the tablespoon of white wine and salt and pepper inside the cavity. In a large saucepan sauté the apples and onions in the butter and oil until they are soft. Add the sauerkraut, blend well with the apple and onions, season lightly with salt and pepper, and mix in the caraway seeds. Simmer over medium heat for 10 minutes. Pour in the ½ cup of wine; bring to a simmer and stir in the grated potatoes. Simmer, uncovered, stirring for 10 minutes. Stuff the cavity of the goose with the sauerkraut mixture; truss it well, rub salt and pepper on it, and place on a rack in a large roasting pan, breast side down. Pierce the skin of the legs, thighs, and wings with a sharp knife to permit the fat to run off. Pour the boiling water over the goose. Place the roasting pan in a preheated 450-degree oven; then immediately turn the heat down to 375 degrees. Roast the goose, uncovered, for 1 hour, basting frequently with the liquid in the pan. Remove the rack from the pan; pour off excess grease and place the goose on its back and roast, basting often, for 30 minutes or until the goose is fork tender.

HASENPFEFFER

GERMANY

Serves 6

- 2 c vinegar
- 1 c dry red wine
- 5 white onions, sliced
- 8 peppercorns, slightly crushed
- 1 t salt
- 4 juniper berries, slightly crushed
- 1 bay leaf
- 1 t allspice
- 2 cloves
- 2 3-lb rabbits, cut up
- salt and pepper
- 5 T butter
- 1 T olive oil
- 1½ c sour cream

In a saucepan combine the vinegar, wine, onions, peppercorns, salt, juniper berries, bay leaf, allspice, and the cloves. Bring to a boil and simmer 10 minutes. Cool. In a bowl place the rabbit pieces, pour the cooled marinade over, and refrigerate for 24 hours. Remove rabbit from marinade; strain the marinade and save. Dry the rabbit pieces with paper towels; sprinkle with salt and pepper. In a large saucepan heat the butter and oil and brown the rabbit evenly. Pour in 2 cups of the marinade, cover the saucepan, and simmer for 30 minutes or until the rabbit is fork tender. Stir in the sour cream; simmer 2 minutes.

RABBIT HOT POT

BELGIUM

Serves 6

- 2 3-lb rabbits, cut up
- salt and pepper
- flour for dredging
- 5 T butter
- 1 T olive oil
- 2 garlic cloves, minced
- 1 medium-sized white onion, thinly sliced
- 3 medium-sized carrots, scraped, thinly sliced
- 2 c dry white wine
- 1 c chicken broth
- 1 c cooked peas
- 12 whole, small Belgian endives, braised in ½ c chicken broth and 2 T butter until tender
- 2 T chopped parsley

Sprinkle the rabbit pieces with salt and pepper. Dredge them with flour. In a casserole heat the butter and oil and brown the rabbit evenly. Pour off fat; add the garlic, onions, carrots, wine, and broth. Bring to a boil on top of the stove; cover and place in a preheated 350-degree oven for 40 minutes or until the rabbit is fork tender. Transfer the rabbit to a hot serving plate. Add cooked peas and endives to the pot and simmer, uncovered, on top of the stove until they are heated through. Taste for seasoning. Spoon the sauce and peas over the rabbit and surround it with the endives. Sprinkle the parsley over all.

RABBIT STEW À L'HORIZON

FRANCE

Serves 6

This recipe, learned from our friend Antoine Gilly, was, in turn, learned by him from a peasant in M. Gilly's home province of Burgundy.

2 3-lb rabbits, cut up
salt and pepper
flour for dredging
5 T butter
1 T olive oil
12 small white onions, peeled, root ends scored
12 ½-inch cubes fatback with streaks of lean through it
2 c dry red wine
1½ c beef broth
2 oz cognac
bouquet garni (3 sprigs parsley, 1 small bay leaf, pinch of dry thyme, 1 celery rib tied in a cheesecloth)
18 small mushrooms, sautéed 1 minute in 3 T butter
2 T chopped parsley

Sprinkle the rabbit pieces with salt and pepper. Dredge them with flour. In a casserole heat the butter and oil and brown the rabbit evenly. Add the onions and the salt pork; sauté for 5 minutes. Cover the pan and simmer for 15 minutes. Pour off the fat. Add the red wine, beef broth, cognac, and the bouquet garni. Bring to a boil on top of the stove; then place, covered, in a preheated 350-degree oven for 20 minutes or until the rabbit is just slightly underdone. Stir in the mushrooms and cook for 10 minutes or until the rabbit is fork tender. Remove the bouquet garni; taste for seasoning. If the sauce is thin, transfer the rabbit to a hot serving plate and reduce the sauce over high heat until it is smooth and thick. Spoon the sauce over the rabbit and sprinkle with parsley.

RABBIT IN VERMOUTH

FRANCE

Serves 6

Vermouth is a wine that becomes vermouth after it is blended with a secret combination of herbs. Few of us realize what a superb cooking liquid it is. Peasants do. We had this dish at a small restaurant in a market village in Burgundy.

1 c flour
1½ t salt
½ t pepper
¼ t dry tarragon
2 3-lb rabbits, cut up
5 T butter
1 T olive oil
2½ c dry white vermouth
1 large garlic clove, minced
2 T chopped parsley

Blend the flour with the salt, pepper, and tarragon and dredge the rabbit pieces. In a fireproof casserole heat the butter and oil and brown the rabbit pieces evenly. Pour off any fat; stir in the vermouth and the garlic, scraping the bottom of the pot. Cover tightly and cook in a preheated 350-degree oven for 40 minutes or until the rabbit is fork tender. Taste for seasoning. Spoon the pan liquid over the rabbit pieces and sprinkle with parsley before serving.

SANDRA HALL'S TURKEY SHORTCAKE

Serves 6

Sandra Hall, daughter of Palmina and Robert Thompson, granddaughter of Maria and Pasquale Limoncelli, follows cooking tradition with high style. She has an imaginative touch with food, sets an impressive table, and is ably aided and abetted by husband, Skip. People snap up their dinner invitations as if they will never get another.

6 T butter
3 c cooked, diced turkey (try for equal portions of light and dark meat)
⅓ c ham, diced
salt and pepper to taste
dash of cayenne
4 T dry sherry
½ c cooked, chopped broccoli
1 c medium cream
3 egg yolks

Melt the butter in a double boiler (over hot water). Stir in the turkey, ham, salt, pepper, and a good dash of cayenne. Add 2 tablespoons of the sherry, blend, and simmer for 2 minutes. Stir in the broccoli and cream and heat until steam forms. Beat the egg yolks with the remaining sherry. Three minutes before serving stir a little hot cream mixture into the egg yolk and sherry mixture; then gradually return this to the pot. Sandra serves this on hot homemade biscuits (no mixes for Sandy!). It can be varied by serving over rice, fluffy mashed potatoes, or fine noodles.

CHAPTER SIX

Meats

Winston Churchill once called peasants "those people who eat well." A countryman of his, essayist and poet William James Linton, was more eloquent. "He boasts nor wealth nor high descent, yet he may claim to be a gentleman to match the best of any pedigree: His blood hath run in peasant veins through many a noteless year; Yet, search in every prince's court, you'll rarely find his peer. For he's one of Nature's Gentlemen, the best of every time."

We hope that when you have finished this chapter and tried a few of "his" recipes, you will have your own eloquent words. To give you creative energy, we recommend Lentils with Cotechino Sausage or *Pasta e Fagioli* alla Pasquale Limoncelli.

CARNE DE VACA ASADA
(Roast Beef)

SPAIN

Serves 6 to 8

2 cloves garlic, minced
1 t salt
½ t pepper
1 t paprika
1 bay leaf
3 c dry red wine
juice of 1 large lemon
1 5-lb top or bottom round pot roast
4 T olive oil
2 T flour

Combine the garlic, salt, pepper, paprika, bay leaf, wine, and lemon juice in a large deep bowl and marinate the beef in this for 7 hours in the refrigerator, turning it several times. Remove from the refrigerator and marinate at room temperature for 2 hours. Drain; strain and save the marinade. Dry the beef with paper towels. In a deep heatproof casserole (just large enough to hold the beef) brown the beef evenly in the oil. Pour off any fat remaining in the casserole and pour the marinade over the beef. Cover the pot and bring to a boil on top of the stove; then roast in a preheated 350-degree oven for 2 hours. Remove the cover and cook for another half hour or until the beef is fork tender. Transfer the roast to a warm serving plate. In a bowl mix the flour with 1 cup of the beef juices and marinade from the casserole. Pour this mixture back into the pot with the remaining liquid. Simmer on top of the stove, stirring, until you have a smooth, thickened sauce. Slice the beef at the table and pass the sauce.

PALMINA THOMPSON'S BEEF PROVINCIALE

ITALY

Serves 6

Palmina Thompson, the youngest daughter of Maria and Pasquale Limoncelli, has the honor of being the most talented of that family of exceptional cooks. She has ten green fingers and can make anything grow, which she then promptly cooks, cans, or freezes. She also is a uniquely organized person who can whip superb meals out of the freezer at a knock on the door. Many of her recipes are adapted from her mother's or are her own. Like her mother, she does magic things with cabbage and can make a simple pork chop sing the "Ave Maria." She, however, is hung up on beef and usually gives it (or veal) first place at her table.

4 T butter
1 T olive oil
3½ lb beef sirloin, cut into 1½-inch cubes
salt and pepper
1 garlic clove, minced
1 (1-lb, 12-oz) can tomatoes, mashed with a spoon
6 medium-sized potatoes, quartered
⅛ t dry oregano
1 package of frozen small peas, defrosted but not cooked

In a large heatproof casserole heat the butter and oil. Season the beef with salt and pepper and brown evenly. Stir in the garlic and then the tomatoes, cover the pan, and simmer on top of the stove for 45 minutes. Add the potatoes and oregano and simmer, covered, 15 minutes or until the beef and potatoes are tender; then stir in the peas, cover, and simmer 3 minutes.

BEEF WITH MASHED POTATOES

HUNGARY

Serves 6

4 T butter
1 T olive oil
3 lb lean beef chuck, cut into 1-inch cubes
12 small white onions, peeled, root ends scored
12 small carrots, scraped and cut in halves
4 T flour
1 T sharp prepared mustard
1 t salt
½ t pepper
1 bay leaf
2 c beef broth
1 c tomato juice
3 c mashed potatoes
2 T melted butter

In a casserole heat the 4 tablespoons of butter and oil and brown beef evenly. Add the onions and carrots to the beef pot. In a saucepan combine the flour, mustard, salt, pepper, bay leaf, beef broth, and tomato juice. Blend well and simmer, uncovered, for 5 minutes. Pour this mixture over the beef and vegetables in the casserole. Cover and cook in a preheated 325-degree oven for 1½ hours or until the beef is fork tender. Taste for seasoning. Remove bay leaf. Arrange the mashed potatoes around the edge of the casserole on top of the beef and vegetables. Dribble the melted butter over the potatoes. Raise the oven heat to 400 degrees and bake beef and potatoes, uncovered, for 15 minutes or until the potatoes are golden.

FOGGIA BEEF ROLL

ITALY

Serves 8 or 10

5 lb top round steak, ground
2 c fine dry bread crumbs
4 leaves fresh basil, chopped (or ½ t of dry basil)
1 T chopped Italian parsley
7 eggs, beaten
1 c coarsely grated Romano cheese
1½ t salt
1 t pepper
1 T olive oil
4 4-inch-long Italian sweet sausages, broiled
4 hard-cooked eggs
4 slices provolone cheese
4 cups tomato sauce
1 t sugar
¼ t ground cinnamon
½ t dried oregano

In a large bowl mix together with your hands the beef, bread crumbs, basil, parsley, beaten eggs, ½ cup of the Romano cheese, salt, and pepper. Spread the olive oil onto a board or clean table where you will make the roll. Reserve 1 cup of the meat mixture for patching the roll later if necessary. Place the rest of the meat on the oiled board. Flatten out into a large square ½ inch thick. Alternate sausages, hard-cooked eggs, and provolone slices on meat so when the meat roll is sliced, each slice will have some sausage, egg, and cheese in it. Sprinkle the remaining grated Romano over everything; sprinkle more pepper and salt. Carefully roll the meat into a firm, tubular roll. If there are holes or open places, patch them with the reserved ground meat. Slide the roll onto an oiled baking pan; bake, uncovered, in a preheated 400-degree oven until it is firm and brown, about 45 minutes. Meanwhile, heat the tomato sauce. Add 2 tablespoons of drippings from the meat pan to the tomato sauce; stir and simmer 5 minutes. Lower the oven heat to 300 degrees. Cover the meat roll with the tomato sauce; sprinkle lightly with sugar, cinnamon, and oregano. Bake, uncovered, for 30 minutes, occasionally basting the roll with the sauce. Transfer the roll to a hot serving dish and let it set for 10 minutes to become firm and slightly cooled for easier slicing.

PFEFFERPOTTHAST
(Pepperpot Stew)

Serves 6

German country folk around Westphalia have preferred these ribs for years, knowing that the meat closest to the bone is the tastiest–and usually the cheapest.

5 lb short ribs, cut in 2-inch pieces
salt and pepper
4 T butter
1 T olive oil
8 small white onions, thinly sliced
2 garlic cloves, chopped
1 bay leaf
2 cloves
3 c beef broth
3 c water
½ c stale pumpernickel bread crumbs
1 T capers, rinsed, drained, and chopped
1 t grated lemon rind (not any of the white part)

Season the short ribs with salt and pepper. In a large casserole heat the butter and oil and brown the ribs evenly. Remove the ribs. Add the onions and garlic, sautéing until the onions are soft. Add the bay leaf, cloves, beef broth, and water; stir well, scraping the bottom of the pot. Put the ribs back into the pot, cover, and bake in a preheated 375-degree oven for 1½ hours or until they are fork tender. Transfer the ribs to a hot serving dish and keep warm. Skim the fat from the liquid in the pot; discard the bay leaf and cloves. Add the bread crumbs, capers, and lemon rind, blending well. Simmer, uncovered, on top of the stove for 10 minutes, stirring often. Spoon this sauce over the short ribs on their serving dish.

POT-AU-FEU

Serves 6

This not only is a French farmer's favorite, usually eaten on Sunday, but also it has become a classic dish, favored by many. On the day it is cooked, the beef and potatoes are eaten, as the potatoes aren't too good reheated. The next day the broth is served as a soup; the next day (and the next) whatever is left is reheated. The tastiness improves day by day.

4 lb beef brisket (shin, shoulder, or chuck)
3 lb beef knuckles
1 tablespoon salt
bouquet garni (2 sprigs parsley, 1 bay leaf, ½ t dry thyme, 6 peppercorns tied in a cheesecloth)
3 medium-sized yellow onions, each stuck with 1 clove
3 garlic cloves, unpeeled
5 qt water
6 celery ribs, scraped and cut into halves
3 small white turnips, scraped and cut into halves
6 small carrots, scraped
3 medium-sized parsnips, scraped and cut into halves
6 leeks, white part only
6 small potatoes
2 T chopped parsley

Place the beef meat, beef knuckles, salt, bouquet garni, onions, garlic, and water in a large deep stock pot (water should come well above the contents of the pot). Bring to a boil; skim the scum that collects from the top. Lower the heat and simmer, partially covered, for 3½ hours or until the beef is almost tender. Add the celery, turnips, carrots, parsnips, leeks, and potatoes and simmer 45 minutes or until the beef and vegetables are tender. Transfer the meat and vegetables (discarding the onions and garlic and bouquet garni) to a hot serving dish and keep them warm. Remove excess fat from the top of the stock. Strain the stock; serve it first with chopped parsley. Serve the beef and vegetables with a horseradish sauce or Dijon mustard and coarse salt.

PALMINA THOMPSON'S BAKED STEAK

Serves 6

This, from the versatile Mina Thompson, was adapted from her mother-in-law's recipe. Her mother-in-law is of Sicilian origin, so this may have been from that island. Mina, however, uses choicer cuts than were recommended for this dish and has added her own touches to a very simple but surprisingly delicious dish.

6 ½-inch-thick steaks from top round, each weighing slightly less than ½ lb, well pounded with a meat mallet
salt and pepper
flour for dredging
4 T butter
1 T olive oil
6 medium-sized potatoes, cut into ¼-inch-thick slices
4 white onions, sliced thinly
2 c beef broth

Sprinkle the beef with salt and pepper and dredge with the flour. In a large frying pan heat the butter and oil and brown the steaks evenly. In a large baking dish arrange a layer of the sliced potatoes, then one of the sliced onions (overlapping the slices, if necessary, to make a single layer); salt and pepper each layer. Spread the browned steaks over the onions (overlapping if necessary). In the pan in which you browned the steaks, stir in the beef broth, scraping the bottom of the pan. Simmer, stirring, 5 minutes. Pour the beef broth over the steaks. Cover the baking dish tightly with a lid or aluminum foil and bake in a preheated 350-degree oven for 45 minutes or until the beef is fork tender.

STEAK AND KIDNEY PIE WITH OYSTERS

SCOTLAND

Serves 6

2 lb round steak, cut into bite-sized pieces
salt and pepper
4 T white onions, minced
2 T minced parsley
flour for dredging
2 slices bacon, coarsely chopped
2 c beef broth
2 veal kidneys (remove and discard membrane, hard core in center, and fat; cut into bite-sized pieces)
2 T butter
1 pt oysters, drained
pastry to cover pie
1 egg yolk, beaten

Pastry

2 c flour mixed with 1½ t salt
⅓ c butter
⅓ c lard
⅓ c cold water

In a bowl mix well the flour and salt, butter, and lard with a pastry blender. Add the water and mix well with a fork. Roll into a ball, wrap in waxed paper, and refrigerate until ready to roll out.

Pie Filling

Sprinkle the beef pieces with salt and pepper and roll in the minced onions and parsley; then lightly dredge with flour. In a casserole arrange the beef pieces in one layer. Sprinkle the bacon over the beef; pour in the stock and cook in a preheated 350-degree oven, covered, for 45 minutes. Meanwhile, dredge the kidneys with flour, season with salt and pepper, and sauté them in the butter for 2 minutes. Add them and the butter in which they were sautéed to the beef pot and continue to cook for 15 minutes or until the beef is fork tender. Transfer contents of the casserole to a deep pie dish, add the oysters, and cover with the pastry that you have rolled out to a ¼-inch thickness. Brush the top of the pastry with the beaten egg yolk and place in a 400-degree oven until the crust is golden (about 30 minutes).

COCIDO
(Spanish Boiled Dinner)

Serves 8 to 10

We have several unique wooden spoons collected from Spanish field-workers and farmers–ranging from an ornately carved one, its bowl twice as large as an open hand, to a delicately scrolled one the size of a serving spoon. The large one is used to dip into a boiled dinner and serve as a plate for the small spoon, the system used when Spaniards eat from the *cocido* pot while working in the field. An old woman usually tends it, keeping the lunch warm by burning straw under the blackened pot. The wooden spoons are handmade and intricate designs and secret symbols are carved on them by the peasants and are highly prized by them–and by us. So is their boiled dinner. Any variety of meats (or fowl) can be used in this recipe, but inexpensive cuts of beef, ham, sausages, and chicken are most popular.

2 lb beef bones
3 lb brisket of beef
6 qt water
1 T salt
1 t pepper
1½ lb lean, smoked ham
½ lb fatback of pork, not salted (labeled in the markets "pork for cooking beans")
8 chorizos (Spanish sausages) or any highly seasoned smoked pork sausage
1 3-lb chicken, cut up
4 leeks (white part and some of the light green part), cut in half lengthwise
8 small carrots
2 garlic cloves
1 large cabbage, cut in wedges, core removed
8 small potatoes
1 can chick-peas, drained
1 cup fine noodles, cooked al dente (slightly chewy) in salted water and drained
2 T chopped parsley

In a deep pot place the beef bones, beef brisket, water, salt, and pepper. Bring to a boil; simmer, uncovered, for 1 hour, skimming any scum from the surface. Add the ham, fatback of pork, and sausages; simmer 30 minutes. Add the chicken and simmer 30 minutes; add the leeks, carrots, garlic, cabbage, and potatoes. Simmer, partially covered, for 30 minutes or until the meats and vegetables are fork tender. (If the chicken and vegetables are tender before the meats, remove them. Return them to heat just before serving.) Stir in the chick-peas and simmer 10 minutes. Taste for seasoning.

Do not spoon right out of the pot as the field hands do, but serve the broth as a first course with the fine noodles and parsley; then present the sliced meats, whole sausages, and chicken on a large hot serving dish surrounded by the vegetables.

The Italians have their own boiled dinner, called *Bollito Misto* (Mixed Boil). They use a variety of meats (beef, veal, pork, chicken, tongue, and *zampone* or *cotechino* sausages) and vegetables in season (peas, beans, broccoli, zucchini), as well as potatoes, cabbage, and so on. They sometimes stuff the fowl before adding it to the pot. All are served on a huge platter for family or guests to make a choice.

ROAST RIBS OF BEEF

ENGLAND

Serves 6

This unique method of roasting standing ribs of beef never fails. That is if you like beef medium rare, very pink, and juicy tender. This, learned in an English farmhouse, had a tasty pairing of Brussels Sprouts with Chestnuts.

1 4-rib beef roast
2 t salt
1 t pepper

Rub the beef well with the salt and pepper. Let it stand at room temperature for two hours. Place it in a roasting pan, fat side up. Cook, uncovered, in a preheated 500-degree oven for 15 minutes for each rib (one hour for a 4-rib roast). Turn the oven off and let the beef remain in the oven for exactly two hours.

During this time *do not open the oven door*. If you do open it to sneak a peek, you'll upset the cooking procedure by letting the heat escape.

SONYA MURPHY'S BEEF AND ZUCCHINI CASSEROLE

Serves 6

Sonya Altman Murphy (her mother is Madeline, the eldest daughter of Maria Cifelli Limoncelli) is one of those fortunates born multitalented. She can paint, sew, teach, manage an office—and cook like a six-armed composite of the best of Italian-French-Chinese chefs. This is a simple but delicious recipe from her repertoire.

3 medium-sized zucchini, diced
¼ c olive oil
salt and pepper to taste
2 small white onions, minced
1 garlic clove, minced
1 lb ground chuck beef
4 fresh mint leaves, minced
¾ c grated Parmesan cheese
½ c bread crumbs
¾ c tomato sauce

Sauté the zucchini dices in the oil until they start to turn golden. Remove with a slotted spoon and drain on paper towels; sprinkle with salt and pepper. In the same pan sauté the onions and garlic until soft; add the ground beef and mint, season, and cook until the meat loses its pink color. In a bowl toss the meat mixture with the zucchini. Add ½ cup of the grated cheese and the bread crumbs and toss again. Transfer to a casserole. Top with the sauce; sprinkle with the remaining cheese and bake, uncovered, 30 minutes in a preheated 350-degree oven or until the top starts to brown.

EASTERN EUROPEAN STUFFED CABBAGE

Serves 6

This is a favorite dish of the peasantry in the Balkans, Poland, Czechoslovakia, Hungary, and even Russia. We like this Hungarian version.

1 large head cabbage	**1½ t salt**
3 T minced bacon fat	**1 t pepper**
4 small white onions, chopped	**pinch of dry thyme**
1 large garlic clove, minced	**1 1-lb can sauerkraut, drained**
½ lb ground veal	**1½ c beef broth**
½ lb ground chuck beef	**1 c tomato puree**
1 c slightly undercooked rice	**2 T butter**
1 egg, beaten	**1 T flour**
1 T sweet paprika	**1 c sour cream**

Pour boiling water over the cabbage to cover and cook 20 minutes. Remove the cabbage, drain, and cool. Carefully separate all the large leaves intact and drain them on paper towels. You'll want 4 or 5 leaves for each person. Cut the tough spine out of the outer, large leaves and cut the leaf through so you'll have 2 smaller "leaves."

In a large frying pan sauté the bacon for 3 minutes. Stir in the onions and garlic; sauté until the onions are soft. Add the veal, beef, rice, egg, paprika, salt, pepper, and thyme; blend well and simmer for 3 minutes. Taste for seasoning. Remove from heat.

Spread the partially cooked cabbage leaves flat, being careful not to tear them. Spoon a tablespoon of the mixture onto each leaf, tuck in the sides, and roll tightly into sausagelike bundles. Toothpicks can be used to secure the rolls. The purpose is to keep the stuffing completely encased in the cabbage leaves.

Line the bottom of a large casserole with the drained sauerkraut. Place the stuffed leaves on top. Blend the beef broth and tomato puree; pour this over the stuffed leaves. Cover the casserole, bring to a boil on top of the stove, and then place in a preheated 350-degree oven for 1 hour.

Remove the stuffed cabbage; keep it warm. In a saucepan melt the butter; blend in the flour to a smooth golden paste. Off heat, stir the sour cream into the paste a little at a time until all has been added and you have a smooth paste. Mix this into the sauerkraut in the casserole. Over low heat, simmer, stirring, for 3 minutes. Do not boil. Place the enriched sauerkraut on a large warm serving dish, bedeck with the stuffed cabbage leaves. Pour the sauce remaining in the casserole into a gravy boat to be served with the cabbage.

SWEDISH MEATBALLS

Serves 6

This recipe, courtesy of Kathryn Kane, a lady most dexterous in garden and kitchen, is a simple but justly famous dish that went from farm to city and country to country.

1 lb lean chuck beef	**¼ c minced onion**
½ lb lean pork	**1 t salt**
½ lb veal	**¼ t pepper**
¾ c zwieback crumbs	**¼ t nutmeg**
1 c medium cream	**2 egg yolks, beaten**
½ c butter	**1 c beef broth**

Grind beef, pork, and veal together 3 times. Soak the zwieback crumbs in cream. Blend well with the ground meats. In a saucepan melt ¼ cup butter and sauté the onions until soft. Add the onions and butter to the meat with salt, pepper, nutmeg, and the egg yolks. Mix well together. Form into balls the size of golf balls and brown in the remaining butter. Add the beef broth, cover the pan, and simmer 1 hour.

A suggestion: In the following veal recipes, except for breast and shank pieces, boned chicken breasts can be substituted if veal is too costly or unavailable.

BREAST OF VEAL CONTADINO

ITALY

Serves 6

3 T butter
2 T olive oil
3 lb veal breast, cut into 1½-inch cubes
salt and pepper
1 medium-sized onion, finely chopped
1 celery rib, scraped and finely chopped
4 medium-sized ripe tomatoes, peeled, seeded, and coarsely chopped
4 leaves fresh basil, chopped, or ¼ t dried basil
1 c beef broth
2 c fresh hulled peas, slightly undercooked, or 1 package of frozen peas, defrosted but not cooked
6 medium-sized mushrooms, quartered, and sautéed in 1 T of butter for 1 minute
2 T chopped parsley

In a casserole heat the butter and olive oil. Add the veal, sprinkle with salt and pepper, and brown it evenly. Remove the veal. Pour off all but 1 tablespoon of fat. Add the onion and celery and sauté for 1 minute. Return the veal to the casserole; add the tomatoes, basil, and broth. Cover, bring to a boil on top of the stove, and place in a preheated 275-degree oven for 1½ hours or until the veal is fork tender. Taste for seasoning. Ten minutes before the veal is done, add the peas and mushrooms with the butter in which they cooked. Stir in the parsley.

STUFFED BREAST OF VEAL GENOVESE STYLE

ITALY

Serves 6

This dish, called *Cima*–famous in Genoa–lifts the less expensive breast of veal into the upper cuisine category. Peasant dishes have a way of doing that.

½ lb lean ground pork
¼ lb prosciutto (Italian ham), minced
1 calf's sweetbread, blanched 5 minutes, chopped
4 slices bread, soaked in milk, squeezed dry
2 T grated Parmesan cheese
½ c cooked, chopped spinach, squeezed dry
1 T minced pistachios
2½ t salt
½ t black pepper
pinch of nutmeg
3 eggs, beaten
1 4-lb breast of veal, boned, trimmed
water
1 large carrot
1 large onion, chopped
1 bay leaf

In a large bowl combine the pork, prosciutto, sweetbread, bread, cheese, spinach, pistachios, 1½ teaspoons of the salt, pepper, nutmeg, and eggs. Spread open the breast of veal (skin side down) and arrange the pork mixture evenly over it. Fold the meat over carefully, skewering or sewing it to keep it in a compact roll that will retain the filling. Tie it in several places with string. Place the veal roll in a casserole just large enough to hold it. Cover with water; add the remaining salt, the carrot, onion, and bay leaf. Cover the pot; bring to a boil on top of the stove; then place it in a preheated 325-degree oven for 1½ hours or until the veal is fork tender. Transfer it to a platter. The Genovese place a heavy weight on top of the veal, giving it a more flat shape. Remove the skewers and strings before serving. It can be served hot or cold.

VEAL SLICES IN CHEESE AND CREAM

NORWAY

Serves 6

We had this dish aboard a diesel ketch in the Arctic Ocean the first night out.

4 T butter
1 T olive oil
6 slices veal from rump, pounded ¼ inch thick, each piece weighing slightly less than ½ lb
salt and pepper
4 white onions, chopped
1½ c sour cream
½ c gjetost cheese (or a sharp cheese of your choice), grated

In a saucepan heat the butter and oil. Season the veal with salt and pepper and brown on both sides. Transfer to a warm dish. Add the chopped onions to the saucepan and sauté until soft. Slowly stir in the sour cream and grated cheese, stirring into a smooth sauce. Return the veal to the pan; cover it with the sauce. Cover the pan and gently simmer for 8 minutes or until the veal is fork tender. Do not boil.

ESCALOPE OF VEAL

FRANCE

Serves 6

6 slices of veal from rump, ¼ inch thick, each piece weighing slightly less than ½ lb
salt and pepper
flour for dredging
5 T butter
½ lb mushrooms, sliced
2 garlic cloves, minced
½ c dry white wine
4 small ripe tomatoes, peeled, seeded, chopped
2 T minced parsley

Sprinkle the veal slices with salt and pepper. Dredge them with flour. In a saucepan melt the butter and brown the veal slices on both sides. In the same saucepan sauté the mushrooms 1 minute. Smother the veal with the mushrooms, sprinkle in the garlic, add the wine and tomatoes, and season with salt and pepper. Cover the saucepan and simmer 15 minutes or until the veal is fork tender. Taste for seasoning. Before serving, sprinkle the veal and mushrooms with parsley.

GULYAS
(Hungarian Veal Stew)

Serves 6

4 T butter
1 T olive oil
4 medium-sized onions, chopped
1 clove garlic, minced
3 lb veal from the leg or rump, cut into 2-inch cubes
1½ T Hungarian paprika
¼ t caraway seeds
1 small bay leaf
pinch of marjoram
pinch of thyme
salt and pepper to taste
1 (1-lb, 12-oz) can plum tomatoes, put through a food mill
2 small red peppers (seeds and white part removed), diced
2 small green peppers (seeds and white part removed), diced
6 medium-sized mushrooms, sliced
1 c sour cream

In a large casserole heat the butter and oil and sauté the onions and garlic until soft. Add the veal cubes and brown evenly. Sprinkle in the paprika and caraway seeds; add the bay leaf, marjoram, thyme, salt, and pepper. Cover and simmer on top of the stove for 5 minutes. Stir in the tomatoes and peppers and place in a preheated 325-degree oven, covered, for 45 minutes. Stir in the mushrooms and cook 15 minutes more or until the veal is fork tender. Stir in the sour cream and simmer on top of the stove, stirring, for 5 minutes. Do not boil. Taste for seasoning.

VEAL WITH GARLIC CLOVES AND RED WINE

FRANCE

Serves 6

3 lb veal from the leg, cut into pieces 1 inch square and ½ inch thick
salt and pepper
4 T butter
1 T olive oil
18 large whole garlic cloves, peeled
3 T flour
2 c chicken stock
1 c dry red wine
1 small bay leaf
pinch of thyme
2 T minced parsley

Salt and pepper the veal. In a casserole heat the butter and oil. Brown the veal evenly; sauté the garlic until golden. Sprinkle the flour over the veal and garlic and shake the pot to distribute the flour. Add the stock, a small amount at a time, stirring, until all is added and the sauce is smooth. Add the wine, bay leaf, and thyme. Mix well; cover and place in a preheated 350-degree oven for 40 minutes or until the veal is fork tender. Sprinkle the veal and garlic with parsley before serving. (Garlic, when braised for some time, becomes sweet and tender.)

VEAL PAPRIKA

CZECHOSLOVAKIA

Serves 6

4 T butter
1 garlic clove, thinly sliced
6 slices of veal, each weighing slightly less than ½ lb, pounded ¼ inch thick with a meat mallet
1 c water
1 pt sour cream
1 T Hungarian paprika
salt to taste

In a saucepan melt the butter and sauté the garlic 3 minutes. In the same pan brown the veal on both sides. Pour in the cup of water, cover pan tightly, and simmer for 20 minutes. Stir in the sour cream, sprinkle the paprika and salt, and stir well. Gently simmer, uncovered, 12 minutes or until the veal is tender. Do not boil.

VEAL PICCATTA

Serves 6

Although this quick and easy dish was created in Italy, other European countries have veal dishes that utilize lemon juice. Veal and lemon are most compatible.

6 slices of veal, cut ¼ inch thick, each weighing slightly less than ½ lb
flour for dredging
salt and pepper to taste
6 T butter
1 T olive oil
1 c Marsala wine
1 lemon, halved, and 3 lemons, quartered
2 T chopped parsley

Place the veal slices between sheets of wax paper and pound with a meat mallet until they are paper thin. Dredge lightly with flour. Season with salt and pepper. In a very large frying pan heat the butter and oil. Over high heat and when the fat is bubbling, sauté the veal 2 minutes on each side. (Do not let the slices overlap when cooking; if necessary, cook 2 or 3 at a time.) Remove from pan and keep veal warm. Pour the Marsala in the pan and scrape the bottom. Simmer, stirring, until it reduces by one-third. Pour this sauce over the veal in its serving dish, squeeze the halved lemon over it, and then sprinkle the parsley over it. Serve with the lemon quarters.

ROAST LEG OF VEAL

POLAND

Serves 8 to 10

1 5-lb leg of veal
2 t salt
1 t pepper
2 garlic cloves, peeled and quartered
juice of 1 lemon
4 T butter
1 T flour
1 c sour cream

Immerse the veal in a pan of boiling water for 2 minutes. According to the Poles, this tenderizes the meat and seals the juices in. Wipe the veal dry; rub well with the salt and pepper. Cut 8 slits in the veal in various places and insert the slivers of garlic. Sprinkle the lemon juice over the meat and let it stand at room temperature for 1 hour. Place on a rack in a roasting pan and rub well with the butter. Roast in a preheated 400-degree oven, uncovered, basting often with pan juices. When the skin begins to brown and crisp, reduce the heat to 300 degrees and cook, covered, 1½ hours or until the meat is almost tender. Combine the flour and sour cream and spread evenly over the veal. Cook, uncovered, for 25 minutes or until the veal is fork tender.

SIMPLE SCALLOPINI OF VEAL

Serves 6

We can't credit any one country with this dish. All Europeans who have calves prepare this dish in some fashion–using wine or stock, according to their own taste. We had this version in Spain.

5 T olive oil
1 garlic clove
6 slices of veal from the leg, cut ¼ inch thick, each slice weighing slightly less than ½ lb
½ c flour seasoned with 1 t salt and 1 t pepper
½ c beef broth
2 T lemon juice
½ c dry sherry
3 T chopped shallots
salt and pepper to taste

In a frying pan heat the oil and brown the garlic. Discard the garlic. Dredge the veal slices with the seasoned flour and brown on both sides in the hot oil. Pour off any remaining oil. Stir in the beef broth, lemon juice, sherry, and shallots, scraping the bottom of the pan. Season with salt and pepper. Cover the pan and simmer for 20 minutes or until the veal is fork tender. Serve the veal with the sauce spooned over it.

OSSI BUCHI
(Braised Veal Shanks)
ITALY

Serves 6

This famous dish even had a special utensil created for it—a long, narrow spoon that slips into the center of the bone to scoop out the marrow. The Italians call the spoon *agente delle tasse*, "the tax collector."

3 veal shanks cut into 2-inch pieces
2 T butter
4 T olive oil
flour for dredging
salt and pepper to taste
pinch of dry rosemary
2 garlic cloves, chopped
2 white onions, chopped
1 carrot, scraped and chopped
1 celery rib, scraped and chopped
2 c dry white wine
1 c tomato sauce
1½ c chicken broth

Tie a string around each piece of shank so the meat won't leave the bone while cooking. Heat the butter and oil in a large casserole. Dredge the veal shanks lightly with the flour; season with salt and pepper and brown them evenly over medium heat. Sprinkle with rosemary, garlic, onions, carrots, and celery. Cover the pot and simmer for 15 minutes. Add the wine, tomato sauce, and chicken broth. Stir well, cover the pot, and cook in a preheated 325-degree oven for 1½ hours or until the veal is fork tender. If necessary, during the cooking, add more chicken broth. This traditionally is served with saffron rice, each serving consisting of a veal shank and a heaping spoon of the rice with the sauce from the casserole spooned over it. But these very special veal shanks cannot be served without *Gremolata.*

Gremolata

1 large garlic clove, minced
2 T minced parsley
1 T grated lemon rind, not any of the white part

Blend the garlic, parsley, and lemon rind together; lightly sprinkle it over each piece of veal shank as you serve it.

VEAL STEW PORTUGUESE STYLE

Serves 6

2 T butter
3 T olive oil
3 lb veal from the shoulder cut into 1-inch cubes
flour for dredging
salt and pepper to taste
1 medium-sized red onion, chopped
2 medium-sized tomatoes, peeled, seeded, chopped
1 c chicken broth
½ c Madeira wine
½ c dry white wine
3 medium-sized potatoes, quartered
12 large, pitted green olives, coarsely chopped
6 anchovies, drained, coarsely chopped

In a casserole heat the butter and oil. Dredge the veal pieces with flour; season them with salt and pepper and brown evenly. Add the onion and cook 5 minutes. Pour off the fat remaining in the pot. Add the tomatoes, broth, Madeira wine, and the white wine. Cover, bring to a boil on top of the stove, and then place in a preheated 350-degree oven for 45 minutes. Scatter the potatoes in the pot and cook 20 minutes or until the veal is fork tender and the potatoes are cooked. Stir in the olives and anchovies. Simmer on top of the stove just long enough to heat them.

VEAL VALDOSTANA
(Stuffed Slices of Veal)

Serves 6

We are not going to apologize for going heavy on Italian veal dishes. The Italians, in our opinion, cook veal better than anyone.

12 slices veal from the rump—cut 4 inches long, 2 inches wide, and ⅜ inch thick—pounded flat with a meat mallet
6 thin slices prosciutto (Italian ham), cut slightly smaller than the pounded veal slices
6 thin slices mozzarella cheese, cut same size as the prosciutto
½ c flour seasoned with 1 t salt and ½ t pepper
6 T butter
1½ c dry white wine

Spread out the slices of veal. Place a slice of ham on 6 of them and then a slice of cheese; cover with another slice of veal. Pound all edges of each combination with the handle end of a knife, sealing the two pieces of veal together. Dredge the veal with the seasoned flour. In a large frying pan heat the butter and brown the veal well on both sides (add more butter if necessary). After all are browned, lower the heat, pour in the wine, and simmer for 15 minutes or until they are fork tender, turning once. At this point the wine should have evaporated mostly and the juices in the pan simmered into a tasty sauce. Spoon it over the veal just before serving.

WIENER SCHNITZEL
(Austrian Veal Cutlet)

Serves 6

This simple veal cutlet created in farm country (in either Austria or Germany—no one is certain) took sophisticated Vienna, all of Austria, and Germany by storm. It may be the most popular meat dish in both countries. A mystique, which attempts to complicate the dish, has sprung up around it. Exactly how hot should the butter in the pan be? Must the veal be marinated in lemon juice first? Should the cutlet be 1⁄16 or ⅛ inch thick? Must it always be from the leg? One thing is certain. Tell your butcher to cut the cutlets from the leg on the diagonal, with the long grain, so they won't fall apart when beaten.

2 T olive oil
2 T water
2 eggs
6 slices of veal, each weighing slightly less than ½ lb
juice of 2 lemons
salt
flour for dredging
1½ c very dry fine bread crumbs
6 T butter
lemon wedges

Beat together in a long, wide, shallow bowl the olive oil, water, and eggs. Place the veal slices between sheets of wax paper and pound with a wooden mallet until each is ⅛ inch thick. Marinate the cutlets in lemon juice for 30 minutes. Drain and sprinkle with salt on both sides. Dredge with flour, shaking off any excess, and dip into the beaten egg mixture; then dredge with bread crumbs. Let stand at room temperature for 30 minutes. In your largest frying pan melt the butter over high heat; reduce to medium heat, making certain the butter is very hot. Drop a crust of bread in it. If it sizzles and cooks quickly, the butter is ready for the cutlets. Cook a couple at a time if the pan is large enough to take them, cooking them 1½ minutes on each side. Turn once. Cutlets should be golden brown. Keep warm in a 250-degree oven until all are cooked. Serve with lemon wedges. The Germans also top Wiener Schnitzel with a couple of anchovy fillets and a fried egg and call it *Schnitzel à la Holstein.*

WEISSWURST (Veal Sausage) AND ONIONS

GERMANY

Serves 6

This is a delicate white sausage, obtainable in any German butcher shop. It is a favorite of the female half of this team.

12 Weisswurst
6 T butter
salt and pepper to taste
6 medium-sized white onions, thinly sliced
flour for dredging
6 oz dry white wine

Prick each sausage in 3 or 4 places. Place in a saucepan with boiling water. Lower the heat and simmer them for 10 minutes. Drain; dry with paper towels. Melt 3 tablespoons of the butter in a saucepan, season onions with salt and pepper, and sauté them until soft and cooked to your taste. Dredge the sausages with flour and brown in another saucepan in the remaining butter. Transfer the sausages to a warm platter. Pour the wine into the sausage saucepan and stir and simmer into a light sauce. Pour this over the sausages, top with the fried onions, and serve with your favorite recipe for mashed potatoes.

LAMB CHIANTI STYLE

ITALY

Serves 6

- **3 T butter**
- **2 T olive oil**
- **3 garlic cloves**
- **3 small onions, chopped**
- **3 lb lean lamb from the leg, cut into 1½-inch cubes**
- **salt and pepper to taste**
- **pinch of dry oregano**
- **pinch of dry rosemary**
- **1½ c red Chianti wine**
- **1 (1-lb, 12-oz) can tomatoes, mashed**
- **2 T chopped parsley**
- **3 celery ribs, scraped, cut into 1-inch pieces**
- **3 medium-sized potatoes, cut into 1-inch cubes**

In a heavy pot heat the butter and oil. Sauté the garlic until brown. Discard the garlic. Stir in the onions and cook for 3 minutes; push aside, add the lamb cubes, sprinkle with salt and pepper, and brown evenly. Pour off any fat remaining in the pot. Stir in the oregano, rosemary, wine, tomatoes, parsley, and celery. Simmer (the liquid should be barely moving), covered, for 35 minutes, stirring occasionally. Add the potatoes. Cook, uncovered, 15 minutes or until the sauce has thickened and the lamb and potatoes are fork tender. Taste for seasoning.

LAMB WITH COUSCOUS

NORTH AFRICA

Serves 6

The peasants from North Africa introduced couscous, a wheat resembling rice but with a nuttier flavor, to Paris and soon had the sophisticated residents of that city literally eating out of their hands. All couscous dishes cooked with meat and spices are called "couscous." They can be complicated with a variety of ingredients, but this is the one we had in Tangier.

4 T butter
2 T olive oil
2½ lb lean lamb from the leg, cut in large cubes
2 small white onions, chopped
salt and pepper to taste
7 c chicken broth
1 bay leaf
½ t ground cumin
¼ t ground ginger
½ c dry chick-peas, soaked in water 5 hours, drained, covered with fresh water, cooked until slightly underdone, and drained
2½ c couscous
½ c raisins, plumped in a little port wine
½ c pignoli (pine nuts), sautéed in butter until crisp

In a heavy pot heat the butter and oil and brown the lamb cubes evenly; add the onions and sauté 2 minutes. Sprinkle salt and pepper over lamb and onions. Add the chicken broth, bay leaf, cumin, and ginger; bring to a boil. Stir in the chick-peas, cover the pot, and simmer for 30 minutes or until the lamb is fork tender. Stir in the couscous and raisins; bring the liquid in the pot to a boil, covered. Remove from the heat immediately and set aside for 10 minutes. Fluff the couscous with a fork. Stir in the pignoli just before serving.

ARMENIAN SHISH KEBAB

Serves 8

This is the oldest way of cooking lamb, and may be the oldest way of cooking, period. Centuries ago tribal warriors speared the pieces of lamb (probably our oldest domesticated animal) with their swords and held them over embers. Today, nomads broil these kebabs over desert campfires. Africans, Asians, and other peoples also cook kebabs and call them by other names. But the recipes were refined in the Middle East. To our way of thinking, the Armenian style is the best.

1 leg of lamb, trimmed of fat and gristle, cut into 1½-inch cubes
4 garlic cloves, cut into halves
1 bay leaf
½ t coriander
½ t ground cumin
1½ t oregano
1½ t salt
1 t pepper
1 c dry red wine
¼ c olive oil
juice of 1 lemon

Place all the ingredients in a bowl, blending well to coat all the lamb cubes. Cover the bowl and refrigerate for at least 6 hours (overnight is better). Place the lamb on skewers, spearing each piece through the center. Broil over a low fire, preferably charcoal, about 5 minutes on each side or until all sides are brown. Caution: Do not overcook. Lamb is always best pink, which means it will be tender and juicy. Overcooked shish kebab is dry and tough with much of its flavor left on the coals. Americans broil onions, peppers, tomatoes, and other things with the lamb pieces. Middle Easterners do not, as the cooking time for lamb, onions, peppers, and tomatoes differs.

IRISH STEW

Serves 6

Lamb could be the best of all stew meats, more tender and flavorful than beef. It sends its aroma into every vegetable that it comes in contact with. Each country has its favorite lamb stew, but probably the most famous is the Irish farmer's. Irish lamb and Irish potatoes seem to have a singular flavor all their own.

3 lb boned lamb shoulder, cut into 1-inch cubes
½ lb bacon, cut into 1-inch pieces
4 large potatoes, cut into 1½-inch cubes
8 medium-sized yellow onions, cut into ¼-inch slices
1½ t salt
½ t rosemary
½ t pepper
2 c water

Place all ingredients in a large pot. Cover tightly; bring to a boil. Then, over low heat simmer for 1½ hours or until the lamb and potatoes are tender, shaking the pot from time to time to prevent the contents from sticking to the bottom.

LAMB WITH PEAS

LEBANON

Serves 6

3 T butter
2 T olive oil
3 lb lean lamb from the leg, cut into 1½-inch cubes
salt and pepper to taste
2 garlic cloves, minced
3 T flour
2 c chicken broth
½ c tomato puree
18 small white onions, root ends scored
½ t cinnamon
2 c hulled fresh peas, slightly undercooked in salted water, or 1 package of frozen peas, defrosted but not cooked

In a deep pot heat the butter and oil; sprinkle the lamb with salt and pepper and brown evenly. Add garlic; sauté 1 minute. Pour off any fat remaining in the pot. Sprinkle the lamb with the flour; shake the pot to distribute it. Stir in the broth, small amounts at a time, until all is used; then blend in the tomato puree. Add the onions and cinnamon and stir. Cover the pot; simmer over low heat for 45 minutes or until the lamb and onions are fork tender, shaking the pot from time to time so contents won't stick. Stir the peas in and simmer, covered, 10 minutes. Taste for seasoning. Serve with hot, cooked bulgur wheat.

KIBBEH
(Ground Lamb with Bulgur Wheat)

Serves 6

The Shemoins Elmirans, from Syria, have cooked this famous Middle Eastern dish for us often. No one can make it as well, but we all can try. It's worth the effort.

½ c bulgur (cracked wheat)
½ c hot chicken broth
1½ lb lean lamb, ground twice
2 small white onions, minced
1 c tomato sauce
1 t salt
½ t ground cumin
¼ t pepper
½ c pine nuts
4 T butter, melted

In a bowl mix the bulgur with the hot chicken broth. Let stand 2 hours. In another bowl place bulgur (it will have absorbed the broth), ground lamb, onions, tomato sauce, salt, cumin, and pepper, blending well. Grease a flat, 9-by-10-inch pan and spread the meat and wheat mixture evenly. Push the pine nuts into the flat meat cake, studding the entire cake; pour the melted butter over it. Cook, uncovered, in a preheated 400-degree oven for 25 minutes.

RACK OF LAMB

FRANCE

Serves 4

Freshness and simplicity are the marks of peasant cookery. It also helps to have a farm and a lamb raised by yourself and then aged to perfection. We had these tender nuggets from a nice pink rack of lamb cooked in a farmhouse in Burgundy. We don't think the cooking method can be improved upon, but you have to like your lamb pink.

1 8-rib rack of lamb
½ t dry rosemary
1½ t salt
1 t pepper

Rub the lamb well with the rosemary, salt, and pepper and let stand at room temperature for two hours. Preheat the oven to 550 degrees. Cook the lamb in a roasting pan, uncovered, for 15 minutes. Lower the oven heat to 400 degrees and cook 12 minutes. Turn the oven off and let the lamb stay for 13 minutes.

ROAST LAMB

GREECE

Serves 6

We continue to comment on the many simple ways country folk have of serving delicious food. This leg of lamb sampled at a farmhouse table on the island of Lesbos is an excellent example of the island's easy but elegant cuisine.

1 5-lb leg of lamb
4 T olive oil
1½ t salt
½ t pepper
4 T butter, melted
1½ c warm tomato juice
1 small stick cinnamon, in pieces

Rub the leg of lamb well with the olive oil, then with salt and pepper. Mix the melted butter, tomato juice, and cinnamon stick pieces in a bowl. Place the lamb in a roasting pan and cook, uncovered, in a preheated 425-degree oven for 20 minutes, basting twice with the tomato juice-butter mixture. Reduce the oven heat to 325 degrees. Pour in the remaining tomato juice-butter mixture, with the cinnamon stick pieces, around the sides of the lamb. Cover the roasting pan tightly and cook for 50 minutes.

LAMB SHANKS WITH ONIONS AND TOMATOES

SYRIA

Serves 6

2 T olive oil
6 lamb shanks
5 small white onions, cut into ½-inch slices
1½ t salt
1 t allspice
½ t mace
½ t pepper
12 small very ripe tomatoes, peeled, seeded, chopped
1½ c beef broth

Pour the olive oil into a fireproof baking dish just large enough to hold the shanks in one layer, coating the bottom well. Arrange the shanks in the dish. Bake in a preheated 425-degree oven for 35 minutes, turning them so they brown evenly. Place the onions in one layer over the lamb; season with the salt, allspice, mace, and pepper. Spoon the chopped tomatoes, in one layer, over the onions. Pour in the beef broth, bring to a boil, cover, and bake in a preheated 375-degree oven for 45 minutes or until the lamb shanks are fork tender. Rice is always served with this.

LAMB SHANKS IN RED WINE

FRANCE

Serves 6

In our view lamb shanks, one of the least expensive lamb cuts, may be the best lamb cut. More importantly, those country people who know best, think so, too, and have devised numerous ways to serve these chunky, tasty items.

4 strips bacon, chopped
6 lamb shanks
1 carrot, scraped and chopped
1 celery rib, scraped and chopped
1 medium-sized onion, chopped
1 garlic clove, chopped
1½ t salt
½ t pepper
2 T flour
1 c beef broth
1 c dry red wine
1 bay leaf
¼ t rosemary
12 small white onions
18 small, fresh mushrooms

In a large casserole sauté the bacon 3 minutes. Add the lamb shanks and brown evenly. Remove the bacon and shanks; stir in the carrot, celery, onion, and garlic. Season with the salt and pepper. Sauté until the vegetables are soft. Stir in the flour, blending it with the vegetables. Return the bacon and shanks to the casserole. Pour in the beef broth and wine, add the bay leaf and rosemary, cover, and simmer for 1 hour. Add the onions and simmer, covered, 20 minutes; add the mushrooms and simmer, covered, 10 minutes or until the lamb shanks are fork tender.

SHEPHERD'S PIE

SCOTLAND

Serves 6

This, from the British Isles, exemplifies in simplicity, economy, and flavor the cunning art of peasant cooking. It is always built around leftover meat, usually lamb.

3 T butter
1 medium-sized white onion, minced
1 T flour
¾ c beef broth
3 c leftover lamb, beef, or veal, cut into small cubes
2 T minced parsley
salt and pepper to taste
pinch of mace
3 c mashed potatoes (mashed with cream and butter)
2 T grated cheese of your choice

In a saucepan sauté the onion in 2 tablespoons of the butter until soft. Stir in the flour; then gradually add the beef broth. Mix in the meat, parsley, salt, pepper, and mace. Butter a 2-quart casserole. Cover the bottom with half of the mashed potatoes. Spoon the meat and onion mixture over the potatoes; then cover with the remaining mashed potatoes. Dot with the remaining butter and sprinkle with the cheese. Bake, uncovered, in a preheated 400-degree oven for about 15 minutes or until completely heated through and brown and crusty on top.

CASSOULET

FRANCE

Serves 8 to 10

This could be the prince of peasant dishes. Of it Anatole France wrote, "Cassoulet has a taste which one finds in the paintings of old Venetian masters, in the amber tints of their women."

1 lb dried, white marrow beans
6 c chicken broth
1 c dry white wine
1 large yellow onion, stuck with 2 cloves
1 large carrot, scraped, cut up
bouquet garni (1 bay leaf, 2 sprigs parsley, 6 peppercorns, ½ t thyme tied in a cheesecloth)
1 garlic clove
2 t salt

Discard any discolored or imperfect beans. Rinse them and soak in water for 5 hours. Drain the beans; place in a deep pot with the chicken broth, wine, onion, carrot, bouquet garni, garlic, and salt. Cover and bring to a boil on top of the stove; then place in a preheated 350-degree oven about 1½ hours or until beans are slightly undercooked–still firm but not hard.

1 4-lb duckling
salt and pepper to taste
1 1-lb garlic sausage (cotechino or a French garlic sausage)
½ lb salt pork
4 T of drippings from duck roasting pan
2 lb (after boning) lean pork shoulder or loin, boned
1 lb (after boning) lean shoulder of lamb (or mutton), boned
2 large onions, chopped
1 c tomato puree
1 c dry white wine
1 c chicken broth
1 c water
bouquet garni (as above with the beans)
1 t salt
½ t pepper
1 c bread crumbs
2 T butter

Sprinkle the duckling with salt and pepper. Roast, uncovered, in a preheated 450-degree oven for 1 hour or until tender. Cool and remove the meat from the bones. Set aside. Reserve the drippings in the roasting pan.

Prick the garlic sausage in several places and place it and the salt pork in a deep pot. Cover with water and simmer, covered, for 1½ hours. Drain and discard the liquid they cooked in.

In a large pot heat the 4 tablespoons of drippings and brown the pork and lamb (or mutton), one at a time. Remove from the pot and set aside. In the same pot sauté the chopped onions until soft. Stir in the tomato puree, wine, chicken broth, water, and the bouquet garni. Add the browned pork and lamb, salt, and pepper; simmer, covered, for 1½ hours or until tender. Remove the pork and lamb. Strain liquid the meats cooked in and reserve.

Cut the duck into bite-sized pieces. Cut the salt pork into thin slices. Remove the skin from the garlic sausage and cut it into slices ¼ to ½ inch thick. Cut the pork and lamb into slices. Drain the beans, saving the liquid. Discard the bouquet garni; strain the liquid and mix it with the liquid the pork and lamb cooked in. Line the bottom of a deep casserole with the slices of salt pork. Then spoon a layer of beans, then a layer of the meat, sausage, or duck. Continue alternating beans and meat, ending with the beans. Heat the bean-and-meat liquid and pour in just enough to come up to the top of the beans (do not cover top layer). Sprinkle top with the bread crumbs and dot with butter. Place, uncovered, in a preheated 350-degree oven for 45 minutes or until top is crusty and brown. Small amounts of the hot liquid may be added if mixture gets too dry. Serve right from the casserole.

CZECHOSLOVAKIAN PORK POT

Serves 6

8 T butter
2 T olive oil
3 lb pork shoulder, cut in 1-inch squares, ½ inch thick
salt and pepper to taste
3 medium-sized yellow onions, cut into thin slices
4 medium-sized potatoes, cut into ¼-inch slices
2 carrots, scraped, cut into slices slightly thinner than the potato slices
2 c finely shredded cabbage (do not use the core)
1½ t caraway seed
2 c hot chicken broth

In a frying pan heat 3 tablespoons of the butter and the olive oil. Brown the pork pieces evenly, seasoning with salt and pepper. Remove pork. Add 2 tablespoons of butter to the frying pan and sauté the onions until soft. Butter a casserole. Arrange layers of onion, potato, and carrot slices and then the cabbage and the pork, making the last layer potato. Sprinkle each layer lightly with salt and pepper and with a little caraway seed. Pour in the hot chicken broth, dot potatoes with the remaining butter, cover pot, and cook in a preheated 375-degree oven for 1 hour or until the vegetables and the pork are fork tender. Serve from the casserole.

FARM-STYLE HAM

GERMANY

Serves 6

We had this as a supper on a farm just outside Munich. It is simple, fast, and delicious. The Germans use goose or chicken fat, but we've tried it successfully with butter and olive oil.

8 T butter
2 medium-sized onions, chopped
4 medium-sized apples, peeled, cored, chopped
1 T olive oil
6 ½-inch-thick slices of bread, crusts cut off
6 slices of precooked ham, slightly less than ½ inch thick, trimmed to the size of the bread slices

Melt 3 tablespoons of butter in a saucepan. Add onions and sauté them for 2 minutes; then add the apples and continue cooking until they are soft. In a frying pan heat 3 tablespoons of butter and the olive oil. Brown the bread on both sides and drain on paper towels. Add remaining butter to the same frying pan and sauté the ham quickly on both sides until it is light brown. Place a slice of ham on a slice of bread and top with apples and onions.

PORK HOCKS WITH SAUERKRAUT

GERMANY

Serves 6

This simple farmer's offering, often cooked after pigs are slaughtered in early winter, is, surprisingly, a favorite of bona fide gourmets such as our friend the late Gaston Lauryssen, a Belgian epicure of note. When he was president of the Carlton House in Manhattan, each Thursday he would go to Luchow's and have pork hocks for dinner. Many times we shared those memorable evenings with him. Interesting, how this prosaic sauerkraut, no matter where eaten, can recall those poetic moments with that sparkling gentleman.

2 T butter
1 T olive oil
2 white onions, minced
2 qt sauerkraut (fresh if available), drained
1 T caraway seeds
salt and pepper to taste
6 large pork hocks, well scraped and scrubbed
warm water
1 medium-sized tart apple, peeled, cored, cut into medium-sized slices

In a large deep casserole heat the butter and oil and sauté the onions until they are soft. Stir in the sauerkraut and blend well with the caraway seeds and the onions. Cover and cook on top of the stove, stirring, for 10 minutes. Sprinkle with salt and pepper. Place the pork hocks in the pot, covering them with sauerkraut. Pour in enough warm water to barely cover the sauerkraut. Cover the casserole and cook in a preheated 300-degree oven for 2 hours. Add the apple slices and cook 30 minutes or until the pork hocks are fork tender. Make flour dumplings and cook them for 15 minutes with the casserole covered.

FLOUR DUMPLINGS

For about 15 dumplings (*depending on the size you like*)

2 c sifted flour
2 t baking powder
1 t salt
⅛ t mace
2 T butter
¾ c milk

Sift the flour, baking powder, salt, and mace together into a large bowl. With a pastry blender cut in the butter until the mixture resembles very coarse cornmeal. Add the milk slowly, stirring it in with a fork until the batter is smooth but as thick as cooked cereal (such as Cream of Wheat)—of a gruel consistency. Dip a tablespoon in cold water each time and scoop out some batter, placing it on top of the simmering sauerkraut. Cover casserole and cook 15 minutes.

KNOCKWURST, PORK, AND SAUERKRAUT

ALSACE-LORRAINE

Serves 6 or 8

4 T butter
1 T olive oil
2 small white onions, chopped
1 garlic clove, minced
1 lb sauerkraut (fresh if available), drained
salt and pepper to taste
½ c dry white wine
12 juniper berries (tied in cheesecloth)
1 t caraway seeds
2 c beef broth
6 smoked pork chops
6 slices thick-sliced bacon
2 tablespoons kirschwasser (kirsch)
6 knockwurst

The Alsatians use goose or duck fat, but we've found that butter and oil work well. In a large casserole heat the butter and oil and sauté the onions and garlic until soft. Stir in the drained sauerkraut. Sprinkle with salt and pepper. Simmer for 10 minutes, stirring the sauerkraut well into the onions and garlic. Pour in the wine; add the juniper berries and caraway seeds; stir well. Pour in enough beef broth to just cover the sauerkraut. Cover the pot and place in a preheated 300-degree oven for 30 minutes. Add the smoked pork chops and bacon, spooning some of the sauerkraut over them. Cook, covered, for 1½ hours. Stir in the kirschwasser, add the knockwurst, and cook for 30 minutes. Discard the cheesecloth with the juniper berries. Traditionally, mashed or plain boiled potatoes are served with this, with everything arranged on one large serving dish.

LENTILS AND COTECHINO SAUSAGES

Serves 6 to 8

This remarkably flavorful dish is cooked in several European countries, using a variety of sausages. This one, which has become a favorite company dish, we discovered in Italy.

1 lb dry lentils
3 1-lb cotechino sausages
2 medium-sized yellow onions, chopped
1 carrot, scraped and chopped
1 celery rib, scraped and chopped
2 garlic cloves, minced
pinch of thyme
5 T olive oil
salt and pepper to taste
about 3 c chicken broth
1 fresh tomato, peeled, seeded, chopped
2 T chopped parsley
1 t paprika

Rinse the lentils and soak them in cold water for 4 hours. Prick the sausages in several places with the sharp point of a knife; place them in a deep pot, cover with water, bring to a boil, cover, and simmer for 2 hours. Let sausages cool in the liquid. Drain lentils and place them in a deep pot with half of the chopped onions, the carrot, celery, minced garlic, thyme, 2 tablespoons of the olive oil, a sprinkle of salt and pepper, and enough chicken broth to cover. Bring to a boil. Simmer, covered, for 30 minutes. Add the chopped tomato and continue to simmer until the lentils are tender but not mushy. Drain the sausage; remove the skin and cut into ½-inch slices. Put these slices into the pot with the lentils. In a frying pan heat the remaining oil; sauté the remaining onions and parsley until the onions are soft. Mix in the paprika and stir into the lentils-and-sausage pot. Taste for seasoning. Simmer, uncovered, for 10 minutes.

LOIN PORK CHOPS (AND SAUSAGE) À LA BOULANGÈRE

FRANCE

Serves 6

We first had this dish with a farmer at a village inn in Burgundy. Sitting at a table washed bone-white by time and energy, drinking local wine while the dish was prepared, we were surprised to see our uncooked lunch in its casserole rushed from the inn to the village bakery. The name of this dish, *boulangère* (meaning "baker's wife"), comes from an old French peasant custom: After the village baker has baked his last loaf of bread, for a small fee his wife will place housewives' casseroles in his oven. These village bakery ovens burned wood and were thought to be the best in the region–the crusty, evenly browned bread a testimonial to that fact.

3 T butter
1 T olive oil
3 garlic cloves, peeled, mashed
6 ¾-inch-thick loin pork chops, pounded lightly with a meat mallet
salt and pepper to taste
6 sweet, fennel Italian sausages (optional, but they give character to the dish)
18 small white onions, root ends scored
3½ c chicken broth
1 large celery rib, scraped, coarsely chopped
1 small bay leaf
pinch of dry thyme
6 medium-sized potatoes, cut into halves

In a large casserole heat the butter and olive oil and brown the garlic lightly. (Two peasant tricks–pounding the pork chops around the bone with a meat mallet and browning the meat first with the garlic.) Season the pork chops with salt and pepper; brown them on both sides. Remove the chops; brown the sausages and remove them. Discard the garlic. Brown the onions. Pour off any fat remaining in the pot. Stir in 1 cup of the chicken broth, scraping the bottom of the pot. Return the chops and sausages to the casserole; add celery, bay leaf, thyme, and the remaining chicken broth. Cover the casserole and place in a preheated 400-degree oven for 20 minutes. Add the potatoes. Cook for 25 minutes. Remove cover, raise the oven heat to 450 degrees, and cook 15 minutes or until the pork, potatoes, and onions are fork tender. Spoon some of the thickened broth over the vegetables and meats when serving.

LOIN PORK CHOPS IN SOUR CREAM

Serves 6

We don't know where this dish originated, but we had it with friends who "raised" their own cream on a farm not far from Geneva, Switzerland.

6 1-inch-thick loin pork chops, lightly pounded with a meat mallet
flour for dredging
4 T butter
1 T olive oil
1 c sour cream
3 T lemon juice
grated rind of 1 lemon, none of the white part
1 t sugar
½ t dry tarragon
salt and pepper to taste
½ c dry white wine

Lightly dredge the chops with flour. In a frying pan heat the butter and oil and brown chops evenly. Place the chops in a single layer in a baking dish. In a bowl blend the sour cream, lemon juice, grated lemon rind, sugar, tarragon, salt, pepper, and the wine. Pour this mixture over the pork chops. Cover the baking dish tightly–first with foil, then with its cover–and bake in a preheated 375-degree oven for one hour or until the pork chops are fork tender.

PORK LOIN EN LECHE

CUBA

Serves 6

1 lean boned loin of pork (or shoulder) weighing 4 lb after being boned
2 T butter
2 T olive oil
salt and pepper
enough warm milk to cover the pork (about 1 qt)

Trim all fat from the pork. Heat the butter and olive oil in a casserole just large enough to hold the pork loin. Brown the pork all around and sprinkle generously with salt and pepper. Pour off any fat remaining in the casserole and cover the pork with the warm milk. Cover the pot and bring to a boil on top of the stove;

then place in a preheated 325-degree oven for 2 hours or until the pork is fork tender. Remove the pork and keep it warm. Strain the liquid in the pot. If it is too thin, cook it down on top of the stove until it thickens. Serve the pork sliced with the milk sauce spooned over it. Good accompaniments are Black Beans, Fried Plantains, and white rice.

PASTA E FAGIOLI ALLA PASQUALE LIMONCELLI
(Pork and Beans and Pasta)

Serves 6

Pasquale, our father and father-in-law, was a man of courage who conquered a strange country with a strange language and made it his. He also conquered the taste buds of anyone who sat at his table. He had the master touch with simple foods, converting the plain into the princely. With this dish he also converted all of his grandchildren and a son-in-law who formerly despised pork and beans into eager devotees.

1 lb dried pea beans
1 3-lb (after being boned) pork loin, boned
2 t salt
½ t pepper
2 garlic cloves, cut into halves
3 T olive oil
bouquet garni (celery leaves from 3 ribs, 1 carrot cut in half, 1 bay leaf, 2 cloves tied in a cheesecloth)
1 (1-lb) can Italian plum tomatoes put through a food mill
2 c ditalini pasta, cooked in salted water al dente (slightly chewy), drained

Discard any dark or imperfect beans and rinse well; cover with cold water and soak for 5 hours. Drain beans. In a large pot place the pork loin with enough water to cover. Bring to a boil, cover, and simmer for 10 minutes. Pour off the water and rinse the pork under cold water. Return it to the pot and cover with fresh water. Add the salt, pepper, garlic, olive oil, and the bouquet garni. Simmer, covered, 1½ hours. Add the tomatoes and beans and simmer, covered, for 1 hour (stirring often but carefully so as not to mash the beans) or until the pork and beans are tender. Remove the bouquet garni. Stir the pasta into the pot; simmer, uncovered, 5 minutes. Taste for seasoning. Serve the pork sliced, with liberal portions of beans and pasta in their broth.

PORK STEW

FRANCE

Serves 6

3 T butter
2 T olive oil
3 lb lean pork from leg or shoulder, cut into 1-inch cubes
salt and pepper to taste
2 T flour
2 c dry white wine
2 c chicken broth
½ bay leaf
pinch of thyme
1 garlic clove, minced
6 slim carrots, scraped and cut into ¾-inch pieces
12 small white onions, root ends scored
2 medium-sized turnips, scraped and cut into 1-inch cubes
1 package frozen Fordhook lima beans, defrosted but not cooked

In a fireproof casserole heat the butter and oil. Sprinkle the pork with salt and pepper and brown evenly. Pour off any fat remaining in the pot. Sprinkle the pork with the flour and stir well to mix. Stir in the wine, scraping the bottom of the pot; add the broth, bay leaf, thyme, and garlic. Cover the pot, bring to a boil on top of the stove, and put into a preheated 350-degree oven for 45 minutes. Add the carrots, onions, and turnips and cook 20 minutes, covered; add the lima beans and cook 15 minutes or until the meat and vegetables are fork tender.

PORTUGUESE PORK WITH CLAMS

Serves 6

This *Ameijoas con Carne de Porco* is a magical mating of pork with seafood, a combination that the Portuguese cook better than anyone. They have a special pan, the *cataplana,* a copper utensil with a lid that almost hermetically seals, giving food a special flavor and moistness. You can't duplicate it, but you can come close by first putting foil over the pan and then covering the pan with its lid.

3 lb (after being boned) pork loin, boned, cut into 1-inch cubes
2 c dry white wine
1½ t salt
1 t pepper
4 T olive oil
salt and pepper to taste
¼ t cayenne pepper
1½ doz littleneck clams, well scrubbed

In a large bowl place the pork, wine, salt, and pepper; marinate 4 hours. Drain and dry pork well; keep 1 cup of the marinade. In a frying pan heat the olive oil and brown pork evenly, seasoning with salt and pepper. In a small casserole with a tight lid, place the pork, sprinkle in the cayenne, and add the marinade liquid that you saved. Bring to a boil on top of the stove; cover with foil, then with the lid. Reduce the heat to a simmer and cook for 45 minutes or until tender. Add the clams, again cover the pot with foil and its lid, and simmer 8 minutes.

SAUSAGES IN BEAUJOLAIS WINE

FRANCE

Serves 6

This simple but tasty dish is a favorite with French farmers, who almost always serve it with a hot potato salad when the new potatoes have just been dug.

12 sausages of your choice, fresh or smoked (we like a combination of sweet and hot Italian)
2 c Beaujolais or any good red wine

If the sausages are fresh, prick them with the sharp point of a knife in several places and sauté them in 2 tablespoons of butter and 1 tablespoon of olive oil for 10 minutes, browning evenly. If the sausages are smoked or dried, they go right into the wine. Cooking time varies according to the size and kind of sausage. Place the sausages and the wine in a casserole, cover, and bring to a boil on top of the stove; then place in a preheated 325-degree oven. Smoked sausages should cook for 20 minutes, fresh for 1 hour.

SAUSAGE WITH TOMATOES

ITALY

Serves 6

3 T butter
2 T olive oil
2 garlic cloves, minced
4 medium-sized onions, chopped
12 sweet Italian sausages
5 large ripe tomatoes, peeled, seeded, chopped
salt and pepper to taste
½ t light brown sugar
2 T chopped fresh basil

In a saucepan heat the butter and olive oil; sauté the minced garlic and the onions until the onions are soft. While the onions are cooking, prick the sausages with the sharp point of a knife and simmer them in water for 10 minutes. Drain and dry. Broil the sausages for 15 minutes, turning often. Add the tomatoes, salt, pepper, and brown sugar to the saucepan with the onions. Simmer, stirring, for 15 minutes or until most of the water from the tomatoes has evaporated. Add the sausages to the tomato-onion sauce and simmer 10 minutes or until the sauce has thickened. Serve with the sauce spooned over the sausages and the basil sprinkled over the sauce.

CHAPTER SEVEN

Variety Meats

It wasn't long ago that many of us disdained calves' brains, beef or calves' livers or hearts, kidneys, sweetbreads, tripe, or even chicken livers. The French call these delicate morsels *abats,* the English call them "offal," and often they are referred to as "variety meats"—which may be the best description of all. They certainly lend variety to a menu. It is soundly established that the country people of our book not only were the first to recognize the taste and vitamin value of these foods, but also they have always placed them in positions of honor in their cooking.

Time has proved the peasant right and, as with many of his foods, has elevated variety meats to the gourmet class, where they are often the first choice of sophisticated cooks. Today sweetbreads are more expensive than prime beef, chicken livers are costly, calves' brains are a discovery, and kidneys are a delight. If you haven't put their "variety" in your life yet, now is the time. If you want something different on your dinner menu that will make the finest steak taste dull, try Veal Kidneys with Brandy and Cream or Baby Beef Liver with Spinach Sauce.

CALVES' BRAINS WITH CAPER AND LEMON SAUCE

Serves 6

We had this dish in Trieste and don't know whether it is Italian or Yugoslavian.

3 sets calves' brains (about 1½ lb)
salt and pepper
flour for dredging
12 T butter
2 T olive oil
3 T lemon juice
3 T capers, rinsed and dried
3 T chopped parsley

Soak the brains in cold water for 2 hours. Drain and rinse. Soak again in fresh cold water with 2 tablespoons of vinegar for 1 hour. Clean the brains, removing the membranes and blood spots. Place them in a saucepan and cover with boiling water. Bring the water to a simmer. Remove from heat; drain and dry. Slice the brains lengthwise; season with salt and pepper. Dredge lightly with flour and shake off any excess so they are barely dusted. In a frying pan heat 6 tablespoons of the butter with the olive oil until the butter bubbles. Sauté the brains until golden on both sides (add more butter and oil if needed). In a saucepan heat together the remaining 6 tablespoons of butter, the lemon juice, capers, and parsley. Mix well and pour over the brains.

LAMB KIDNEYS, MUSHROOMS, AND MADEIRA

PORTUGAL

Serves 6

12 lamb kidneys, membranes peeled off, fat and hard core in center removed, and cut into ¼-inch-thick slices
salt and pepper
flour
4 T (½ stick) butter
1 T olive oil
1 large garlic clove, mashed
½ lb small, fresh mushrooms, sliced
5 oz Madeira wine
2 T chopped parsley

Sprinkle the kidney slices with salt and pepper. Dust lightly with flour. In a large frying pan heat the butter and oil; quickly brown the slices on both sides with the garlic. (Do not overcook the kidneys; they should be pink inside.) Remove with a slotted spoon, discarding the garlic, and keep warm. Add the mushrooms to the same pan, season with salt and pepper, and sauté 3 minutes or until they are tender but still firm. Return the kidney slices to the pan; pour in the Madeira wine and simmer 2 minutes or until most of the wine has cooked off. Taste for seasoning. Serve with the parsley sprinkled on top.

LAMB KIDNEYS WITH MUSTARD

FRANCE

Serves 6

12 lamb kidneys, membranes peeled off, fat and hard core in center removed, and cut into halves
5 T butter
salt and pepper
2 garlic cloves, chopped
½ lb fresh mushrooms, sliced
2 T Dijon mustard
2 t tomato paste
2 T flour
½ c dry red wine
1 c beef broth
1 small bay leaf
1 T chopped chives
1 T chopped parsley

Dry the kidneys. In a saucepan heat the butter; add the kidneys, sprinkle with salt and pepper, and quickly brown them. Remove the kidneys and keep them warm. In the same pan sauté the garlic 2 minutes, add the mushrooms, and sauté 2 minutes. Stir in the mustard, tomato paste, and flour, mixing well. Stir in the wine and beef broth. When blended, add the bay leaf and return the kidneys to the pan. Simmer, stirring, for 10 minutes or until the kidneys are tender but still pink inside (do not overcook as the kidneys will toughen). Serve with the chives and parsley sprinkled on top.

VEAL KIDNEYS WITH BRANDY AND CREAM

ITALY

Serves 6

1 medium-sized white onion, chopped
3 T butter
2 T olive oil
4 or 5 (depending on their size) veal kidneys, membranes peeled off and fat removed, cut into large dices
salt and pepper
3 oz brandy
1 c heavy cream
½ lb fresh mushrooms, sliced and sautéed in 3 T of butter for 3 minutes

In a frying pan sauté the onion in 1 tablespoon of the butter and 1 tablespoon of the olive oil until soft. Add remaining butter and oil. When hot, add the kidneys, season with salt and pepper, and sauté them quickly until they are brown on the outside but still pink inside. Remove with a slotted spoon and keep warm. Pour the brandy and cream into the frying pan and simmer until the pan liquid has reduced by one-half. Stir in the mushrooms; return the kidneys to the pan and simmer 2 minutes (do not overcook as the kidneys will toughen). Taste for seasoning.

VEAL KIDNEYS IN RED WINE

HUNGARY

Serves 6

4 or 5 (depending on their size) veal kidneys, membranes peeled off and fat removed, cut into ¼-inch-thick slices
½ c flour seasoned with 1 t salt and ½ t pepper
4 T butter
2 T olive oil
1 medium-sized white onion, chopped
1½ c dry red wine
salt and pepper to taste
2 T chopped parsley

Dredge the kidney slices lightly with the seasoned flour; shake off any excess so they are barely dusted with flour. In a large frying pan heat the butter and oil; add the kidneys and quickly sauté them until they are brown on the outside and still pink inside. Remove and keep warm. Sauté the onion in the same pan until it is soft. Pour in the wine and simmer for 3 minutes or until the pan liquid has reduced by one-half and has thickened. Return the kidneys to the pan and simmer for 2 minutes (do not overcook as the kidneys will toughen). Taste for seasoning. Serve with the parsley sprinkled on top.

BABY BEEF LIVER WITH SPINACH SAUCE

DENMARK

Serves 6

6 ⅜-inch-thick slices (about 1½ lb) baby beef liver, trimmed
½ c flour seasoned with 1 t salt and ½ t pepper
2 eggs, beaten
1 c bread crumbs
6 T butter
2 T olive oil
3 shallots, minced
1½ c beef broth
juice of 1 lemon
4 T chopped, fresh spinach

Dredge the liver with the seasoned flour; shake off any excess so that liver is barely dusted; dip in beaten egg; dredge with bread crumbs. In a large frying pan heat 4 tablespoons of the butter and the olive oil. Sauté the liver until brown on both sides but pink inside (about 3 minutes on each side). Remove and keep warm. Pour off any fat remaining in the pan. Add 2 tablespoons butter to the same pan, add the shallots, and sauté until they are soft. Stir in the beef broth, lemon juice, and spinach; simmer for 3 minutes or until the liver has reduced by one-half and has thickened. Taste for seasoning and serve the sauce over the liver slices.

CALVES' LIVER WITH SHERRY

SPAIN

Serves 6

- 3 slices bacon, cut in half to make 6 short slices, cooked until transparent, drained
- ½ lb small fresh mushrooms, sliced, sautéed in 3 T butter for 2 minutes
- 6 thin slices (about 1½ lb) calves' liver, trimmed, cut into halves to make 12 small slices
- salt and pepper
- 6 T butter
- 2 T olive oil
- 1 large white onion, chopped
- 2 T flour
- 1½ c beef broth
- ½ c dry sherry
- 2 T chopped parsley

Prepare bacon and mushrooms; set aside. Sprinkle the liver with salt and pepper. In a large frying pan heat 4 tablespoons of the butter and the olive oil. Add the liver and brown lightly on both sides (about 1 minute on each side). Remove and keep warm. Pour off any fat remaining in the pan. Add the 2 remaining tablespoons of butter to the same pan. Sauté the onion until soft. Sprinkle in the flour and stir to mix well. Pour in the beef broth and sherry, small amounts at a time, stirring until all is added and you have a smooth, medium sauce. Stir in the bacon slices and mushrooms. Return the liver to the pan and simmer 5 minutes or until the liver is cooked but still pink inside (do not overcook as the liver will toughen). Taste for seasoning. Serve with the parsley sprinkled on top.

CALVES' LIVER AND SOUR CREAM

GERMANY

Serves 6

- 1½ lb calves' liver, cut into ⅜-inch-thick slices
- salt and pepper
- flour for dredging
- 5 T butter
- 1 medium-sized onion, chopped
- 1 c beef broth
- pinch of dry thyme
- ½ c sour cream
- 2 T vinegar

Cut the slices of liver into strips ½-inch wide. Season with salt and pepper. Dredge with flour, shaking off any excess so that slices are barely dusted. In a large frying pan heat 2 tablespoons of the butter and sauté the onion until it is soft. Add the remaining butter. When it is hot, add the liver strips and lightly brown them on both sides (about 1 minute on each side). Mix in the beef broth and thyme. Cover and simmer for about 3 minutes or until the liver is cooked but still pink inside (do not overcook as the liver will toughen). Stir in the sour cream and vinegar and heat to a simmer. Taste for seasoning.

CHICKEN LIVERS WITH SAGE

ITALY

Serves 6

- 6 slices of bread, crusts removed, fried in butter until golden on both sides, drained on paper towels, and kept warm
- 1½ lb chicken livers, each cut into 2 or 3 pieces
- salt and pepper
- 5 T butter
- 2 T olive oil
- 3 thin slices prosciutto (Italian ham), coarsely chopped
- 1 c Marsala wine
- 2 T chopped, fresh sage

Prepare the bread; set aside. Season the chicken livers with salt and pepper. In a large frying pan heat 3 tablespoons of the butter and the olive oil; add the livers and sauté them until they are well browned on both sides but still pink inside (do not overcook as the livers will toughen). Remove the livers and keep them warm. Add the prosciutto to the frying pan and cook 1 minute. Remove and keep warm with the livers. Pour the Marsala into the pan, add the sage, and simmer, stirring, until the liquid has reduced by one-half. Return the livers and the prosciutto to the pan, stir in the remaining butter, and simmer just long enough to heat the livers and prosciutto through and melt the butter. Taste for seasoning. Serve on the fried bread.

SWEETBREADS AND PEAS

ITALY

Serves 6

Sweetbreads, the thymus glands of young animals, have a remarkably delicate flavor and should not be overwhelmed with strong spices and seasonings. The best recipes are the simplest ones. We remember sampling, in a fanfare restaurant in Florence, sweetbreads that were swimming in tomatoes, garlic, onions, a couple kinds of wine, prominent herbs, and much lemon—really a superior sauce. In fact, it was so superior that all you could taste was the sauce; the personality of the sweetbreads was diminished to the point where they could have been called herring and we wouldn't have known the difference.

3 pairs sweetbreads, soaked for 1 hour in cold water with 1 T lemon juice (add ice to the water to keep it cold)
1 t salt
2 T lemon juice
4 T butter
⅔ c dry white wine
2 T flour
1½ c chicken broth
2 T chopped parsley
3 c of peas (fresh or frozen), cooked in 2 T of butter and 1 c of chicken broth until tender

Drain the sweetbreads. Place them in a saucepan; cover with boiling water. Add the salt and lemon juice and simmer for

15 minutes. Drain and plunge into ice water to cool. Drain and carefully remove and discard all membranes and tubes connecting the lobes. Dry well. In a frying pan heat the butter and lightly brown the sweetbreads on both sides. Pour in the wine and simmer until most of the liquid has evaporated. Remove the sweetbreads and keep them warm. Stir the flour into the pan and add the broth—a small amount at a time until you have a smooth sauce. Return the sweetbreads to the pan, cover, and simmer for 20 minutes (do not overcook as the sweetbreads will toughen). Taste for seasoning. Stir in the parsley. Serve the sweetbreads and sauce with a border of the peas.

TRIPE WITH TOMATOES

SPAIN

Serves 6

Tripe is the stomach lining of a cow. It is one of four stomach linings, each having its own market name. The most palatable, to our taste, is the second stomach, or honeycomb tripe. Few have tasted tripe, and most Americans who dote on the more recognizable parts of the beef critter will stick up their noses at tripe. They shouldn't. It is delicious, and at a time when even the lowly hot dog is expensive, tripe is an excellent family buy. We had this particular dish in Spain, but versions much like it are also popular in France, Greece, and Italy.

3 lb fresh white veal honeycomb tripe
3 T olive oil
3 T chopped salt pork
1 garlic clove, minced
1 lemon, cut into 1-inch-thick slices
1 (1-lb, 12-oz) can plum tomatoes, mashed
scant ½ t dry oregano
1 bay leaf
1 t salt
½ t black pepper
¼ t crushed dry red pepper

Wash the tripe carefully in several waters. Place the tripe in a large pot, cover with 4 quarts of water, and simmer, covered, for 3 hours or until tender. Pour off the water twice during the boiling and replace with fresh hot water. Drain the tripe well, cool, and cut into ½-by-2-inch pieces. In a deep saucepan heat the olive oil and sauté the salt pork and garlic for 6 minutes. Add the lemon slices, tomatoes, oregano, bay leaf, salt, black pepper, red pepper, and the tripe pieces. Simmer, uncovered, for 25 minutes until the sauce has thickened. Taste for seasoning. Discard the lemon slices and bay leaf. This can be served with rice, pasta, or tiny new boiled potatoes.

CHAPTER EIGHT

Pasta, Rice, and Other Grains

Any self-respecting peasant can make a meal out of pasta, rice, or other grains, his technique learned from many years of making do with what he had on hand. Pasta with nothing but butter or olive oil and black pepper can be very tasty, as can rice; polenta boiled and then fried is fine; plain kasha has sustained many a Russian farm family through a hard winter. But, normally, pasta and rice are paired with meats or seafoods to make a complete, well-balanced meal. These two, plus other grains, are served with stews and game and fowl as an appetizing substitute for potatoes and even bread. The ways these wheats and grains are cooked and served are infinite, again limited only by the imagination of the country people. Here, we have tried to offer a significant sampling that will appeal to *your* imagination.

BULGUR PILAF WITH CURRANTS AND PINE NUTS

EGYPT

Serves 6

Long before man learned to grind wheat into flour, he boiled it in open kettles and then spread it in the sun to dry. The nutty, nutritious result was bulgur, staple table fare in the Near East.

2 T butter
1 T olive oil
2 small white onions, minced
2 c uncooked bulgur (cracked wheat)
4 c chicken broth
⅛ t cinnamon
1½ t salt
3 T currants, sautéed until crisp in 1 t butter
3 T pine nuts, sautéed until crisp in 1 t butter

In a saucepan heat butter and oil. Add the onion and sauté over medium heat until soft. Stir in the wheat; sauté 2 minutes. Add the chicken broth and cinnamon, bring to a boil, cover pan, lower heat, and simmer 20 minutes or until the liquid has been absorbed and the wheat is tender. Season to taste with salt; then fluff the wheat with a fork. Blend in the crisp currants and pine nuts. This is usually served with lamb or chicken.

QUICK COUSCOUS

NORTH AFRICA

Serves 6

Another Near Eastern favorite, very popular with the Arabs (see meat chapter), is couscous. It has a very nutty concentrated wheat flavor and is usually cooked with lamb and eaten with the fingers. We suggest a fork.

4 c boiling water
1½ t salt
2 c couscous
4 T butter

In a pot keep water at a boil, add salt, and stir in the couscous. Stir in butter and lower heat. Simmer for 5 minutes, stirring, until water is almost absorbed. Remove from the heat, cover the pot tightly, and let stand for 15 minutes. Fluff with a fork before serving.

KASHA

RUSSIA

Serves 6

Kasha, or groats, is similar to bulgur but much more coarsely ground. It has a most unusual flavor and will have guests asking questions.

3 c kasha	**6 T butter**
3 eggs, beaten	**1½ t salt**
6 c hot chicken broth	**½ t pepper**

Place the kasha in a casserole and blend the beaten eggs into it, coating each grain. Place over very low heat and cook, stirring, just until the grains are glazed. Still on the low heat, stir in the hot chicken broth, a small amount at a time, blending it well into the kasha. Make a well in the center, add the butter, fluff up the kasha, and add salt and pepper to taste. Cover the casserole and place in a preheated 300-degree oven for 40 minutes or until the kasha is tender and fluffy.

LINGUINE WITH WHITE CLAM SAUCE

Serves 6 or 8

This dish was concocted by Italian fishermen—as were so many other superior dishes, such as their marinara sauce and *Zuppa de Pesce*. Fresh clams were used, but since they aren't always available, we've run several experiments with canned minced clams. Surprisingly, the canned clams produced the better sauce each time. Too often fresh clams become rubbery. We also discovered that the secret of the sauce was in cooking down the clam juice into almost an essence. The Italians, masters with any pasta, always use linguine (a flat spaghetti) with any type of seafood. Exactly why, no one seems to know.

- **3 T olive oil**
- **3 cloves garlic, mashed**
- **4 (8-oz each) bottles clam juice**
- **4 (8-oz each) cans minced clams**
- **2 cloves garlic, minced**
- **salt and pepper to taste**
- **½ t crushed hot red pepper (optional)**
- **2 lb linguine**
- **5 T butter**
- **4 T fresh parsley, minced**

In a deep saucepan heat the oil and sauté the 3 cloves of garlic until brown. Discard the garlic. Take pan from heat, as the next step would make the hot oil splatter. When the oil has cooled a little, pour in the clam juice. Drain the liquid from the minced clams, set the clams aside, and add their liquid to the pan with the bottled juice. Add the 2 cloves of minced garlic, salt, and pepper, remembering that clam juice is somewhat salty. If you use red pepper, as the Italian fishermen do, sprinkle it into the clam juice. It adds authority. Over medium heat, uncovered, reduce the sauce to slightly less than half. In boiling salted water cook the linguine *al dente* (slightly chewy). Drain it and place it in a hot bowl with the 5 tablespoons of butter cut into pieces. Toss the pasta well in the butter. Stir the minced clams that were set aside into the hot sauce. Remove from the heat. Spoon half of the sauce onto the linguine in its hot bowl; toss well. Add the parsley; toss well again, working fast to keep everything hot. Serve in hot rimmed soup bowls with the remaining clam sauce spooned on top of each serving.

MACARONI À LA CREME
(Macaroni and Cream)
FRANCE

Serves 6

- **1 lb elbow macaroni**
- **5 T butter**
- **1 c boiled ham, minced**
- **3 egg yolks**
- **1 c heavy cream**
- **¼ t nutmeg**
- **1 c grated Gruyère cheese**
- **salt and pepper to taste**

Cook the macaroni in boiling, salted water until it is *al dente* (slightly chewy, not too soft). Drain. In a saucepan melt the butter and gently stir in the macaroni until it is well coated with butter. Blend in the ham. Beat the egg yolks with the cream and nutmeg. Stir the egg yolk-cream-nutmeg mixture into the macaroni; then blend in the cheese. Taste for seasoning, adding salt and pepper if needed. Heat through.

POLENTA
(Cornmeal Pudding)

Serves 6

This is often served instead of pasta or potatoes in some sections of Italy, and it is especially good with stew-type meat dishes that have been cooked in a tomato base.

2 t salt
5 c boiling water
2½ c yellow cornmeal
5 T butter
1 c grated Parmesan cheese

Add salt to the boiling water. Stir the cornmeal slowly into the boiling water, keeping the water boiling. Reduce heat and simmer the cornmeal for 30 minutes, stirring almost constantly so that it won't stick and burn. When finished, the spoon will stand upright in the thick, smooth mush. Stir in the butter and cheese, blending well. Cover the pot, remove from the heat, and let stand for 10 minutes.

BAKED RICE WITH CHEESE AND TOMATOES

SWITZERLAND

Serves 6

4 T butter
3 white onions, minced
1 garlic clove, minced
2 ripe tomatoes, peeled, seeded, chopped
1½ c rice
1 t salt
¼ t dry thyme
1 small bay leaf
1½ c chicken broth
4 T grated Swiss cheese
3 T grated Parmesan cheese

In a casserole melt butter and sauté onions and garlic until soft. Stir in the tomatoes, rice, salt, thyme, and bay leaf, blending well. Pour in the chicken broth, stirring. Cover casserole, bring to a boil, and place in a preheated 400-degree oven for 15 minutes. Remove cover, discard bay leaf, stir in the two cheeses, and heat in the oven for 2 minutes.

MARIA CIFELLI LIMONCELLI'S RICE WITH EGG, LEMON, AND CHEESE

Serves 6

3 T butter
3 c cooked rice
juice of 1 lemon
3 eggs
½ c grated Parmesan cheese

In a saucepan melt butter; stir in the rice, fluffing it up with a fork and heating it through. Lower heat. In a bowl beat lemon juice, eggs, and cheese together. Blend this mixture thoroughly with the hot rice. Cook, stirring until the eggs begin to set.

PORK FRIED RICE

CHINA

Serves 6

2 whole eggs
4 T soy sauce
½ t monosodium glutamate
¼ t ginger
2 T peanut oil
1½ c lean raw pork, cut in ½-inch dices
2 cloves garlic, minced
5 whole, small scallions
3½ c cooked rice

In a bowl beat together the eggs, monosodium glutamate, soy sauce, and ginger. In a saucepan heat oil and brown pork evenly; lower heat and cook, stirring (stir-frying) until pork is fork tender. Add the garlic and sauté until soft. Slice thinly, on a slant, the white part of the scallions and then the green tails. Add the white part to the pork and garlic, stir-frying for 3 minutes; then add the green parts and cook 2 minutes. Both should be crisp. Stir in the cooked rice. When hot and well blended with the pork, add the beaten egg mixture. Stir-fry until eggs are set.

RICE STUFFING FOR FOWL

To stuff two birds

This was discovered in a simple country inn near Bologna, Italy. A pair of pheasants had been stuffed with it, but it makes any bird exotic. It's a table-talk recipe that will make guests garrulous.

2 sweet Italian sausages, casings removed, ground meat half-cooked, drained of fat
3 T chopped onions, sautéed in 2 T butter until soft
3 c cooked rice
3 T grated Parmesan cheese
2 eggs, beaten
¼ t oregano
⅛ t dry basil
salt and pepper to taste

In a bowl combine all ingredients. Mix well with a fork; do not mash them together. Spoon the mixture into the cavities of the birds to be roasted. Do not jam it in. Truss each bird and roast your own way. In Italy that splendid Avorio rice from the Po Valley was used as the base, but any good long-grained rice works well.

RUMANIAN NOODLES

Serves 6

½ lb ground beef, cooked
1 lb ground pork, cooked
2 small slices white bread, crusts removed, soaked in chicken broth, liquid squeezed out
2 small white onions, minced
⅓ c fresh parsley, chopped
½ t dry fennel
salt and pepper to taste
3 eggs
1 c heavy cream
½ c grated Romano cheese
1 lb noodles, cooked al dente, slightly underdone
4 T butter

Blend together the cooked beef, cooked pork, bread, onions, parsley, fennel, salt, and pepper. Beat the eggs, cream, and cheese together to blend thoroughly. In a buttered baking dish arrange a layer of noodles, then one of the beef-and-pork mixture, making the top layer noodles. Pour the egg mixture over the top layer of noodles. Dot with butter and cook, uncovered, in a preheated 375-degree oven for 40 minutes or until golden on top.

SPAGHETTINI ESTIVI

Serves 6

This pasta dish, with its unusual uncooked sauce, is served in only a few rural areas in Italy, and then only in summer, when the tomatoes are ripe and the basil is fresh.

6 medium-sized, very ripe tomatoes, peeled, seeded, chopped
6 large, fresh basil leaves, chopped
3 T chopped broad-leafed Italian parsley
juice of 1 large lemon
4 T olive oil
2 cloves garlic, minced
1½ t salt
½ t pepper
1½ lb spaghettini, cooked al dente

Place a strainer over a bowl and strain the chopped tomatoes for 20 minutes to get rid of excess moisture. In a mixing bowl place strained tomatoes, basil, parsley, lemon juice, olive oil, garlic, salt, and pepper. Toss everything well with a pair of spoons; then let the mixture stand at room temperature for 1 hour. The cooked pasta must be hot, right from the water, and should be served in hot bowls. Toss the pasta with half of the sauce and spoon the remaining sauce over the individual portions.

SPAETZLE

GERMANY

Serves 6

These little noodles are excellent with any dish that has a rich gravy or sauce or with lusty soups.

3 c flour
2 t salt
3 small eggs, beaten
1 c water (for richer noodles, use milk)

In a bowl sift flour and salt. Stir in the eggs and blend, adding water slowly until the mixture is stiff and yet smooth. Flour a board and press the dough flat on it. Using a very sharp knife, slice off small pieces of dough. Another method is to press the dough, a few tablespoons at a time, through the large holes in a colander, directly into the boiling water. With either method the spaetzle should be cooked in 2 quarts of boiling water to which 1 teaspoon of salt has been added. Cook a few at a time, stirring so they don't stick together. Cook for 5 minutes or until the noodles are done to taste; then drain before serving. If served as a side dish, they are improved if drenched in hot melted butter.

MARION LOVING'S GRANDMOTHER'S SPOON BREAD

Serves 6

We are breaking our theme here to offer an American recipe from a Virginia friend. But this is so delicious served with sausage cakes or bacon and so poetic with red-eye gravy and country ham slices that it would be sacrilegious to omit it from this chapter.

2 eggs, beaten until light
1 c milk
1 c buttermilk
⅓ c white cornmeal
2 t baking powder
½ t baking soda
½ t salt
2 T melted butter

In a bowl beat eggs; stir in the milk, buttermilk, cornmeal, baking powder, baking soda, salt, and butter. Blend all together very well. Butter a casserole and pour the mixture into it. Bake, uncovered, in a preheated 450-degree oven for 30 minutes. When cooked properly, it is custardlike but light.

SIMPLE YORKSHIRE PUDDING

ENGLAND

Serves 6

1 c flour, sifted	**2 eggs, well beaten**
½ t salt	**½ c water**
½ c milk	**½ c butter, melted**

All ingredients must be room temperature. Place sifted flour and salt in a bowl; spoon a well in the center, pour in the milk, and mix it well into the flour. Stir the beaten eggs into the flour mixture and beat into a smooth batter. Now beat the water into the batter well, beating constantly until large bubbles rise. Cover the bowl and refrigerate for 1 hour. Beat very well again. Muffin tins are ideal for cooking the pudding. The tins should be hot. One-quarter of an inch of hot melted butter should be spooned into each muffin circle. Pour in the batter to a depth of ⅝ inch. Bake in a preheated 425-degree oven for 15 minutes. Reduce heat to 350 degrees and bake for another 20 minutes or until pudding peaks and is dark golden brown and very light. This is excellent with roast beef or any roast.

CHAPTER NINE

Vegetables

People of the soil, to whom this book is dedicated, have more respect for the earth and what grows from it than anyone. That, of course, is an understatement. The soil is their lifeline. For most of us, though, vegetables hard-won from that soil are more or less taken for granted. We mash, bake, or boil potatoes; we halfheartedly mix peas and carrots together; we cook broccoli and, perhaps in a burst of creative energy, flavor it with butter and lemon. But, mainly, too many of us treat vegetables with less respect than we should, believing that they are necessary to balance our vitamin intake and serving them more out of habit than belief in their versatility.

Here (one caution–try to buy *fresh* vegetables in season!) we have tried to select unique peasant recipes that we have found in various sections of the world that will help relieve the monotony of your vegetable offerings.

ARTICHOKES (STUFFED)

ITALY

Serves 6

6 medium-sized, crisp, green artichokes
8 slices bread, crusts removed, broken into very small crumbs
4 T walnuts, finely chopped
4 T raisins, finely chopped
1 clove garlic, finely minced
2 T parsley, finely minced
3 T olive oil
salt and pepper to taste

Cut off, trim, and finely chop the stems of the artichokes. Remove the small outside leaves around the base of the artichokes and cut off the top third. With your hands, with the open side of the artichoke up, work the leaves loose to separate them, but do not break them off. Remove the center yellow leaves; then remove the fuzzy part on the bottom with a spoon. Wash artichokes well, letting water run between the leaves. Drain them bottom side up; then lightly salt the inside. In a bowl combine the chopped stems, bread crumbs, walnuts, raisins, garlic, parsley, olive oil, salt, and pepper. Mix well with a fork. Drop a small amount of this stuffing between the leaves, starting with the outside leaves. When all of the stuffing has been used, set the artichokes in a baking dish just large enough to hold them snugly. Pour ½ to 1 inch of hot water into the baking dish, cover, and bake in a preheated 350-degree oven 35 minutes or until the leaves can be pulled off easily.

ALCACHOFAS Y JUDIAS
(Artichokes and Green Beans)

SPAIN

Serves 6

- **1 package frozen artichoke hearts, cooked according to directions on package, drained**
- **1 pound small fresh green string beans, cooked in salted water until tender but still crisp, drained**
- **4 thin slices prosciutto (Italian ham), chopped**
- **4 slices bacon, cooked crisp, drained, chopped**
- **2 T parsley, chopped**
- **2 T olive oil**
- **salt and pepper to taste**

In a deep saucepan combine all of the ingredients. Blend well. Simmer 5 minutes and serve. This also may be served as a first course.

FRIJOLES NEGROS
(Black Beans)

Serves 6

This recipe was cooked for us by a weekend guest who was, at the time (before Castro), the Spanish attaché to Cuba. He said it was a Spanish dish. Perhaps he was more influenced by the Cubans than he realized–his companion was a most attractive young lady from Havana and a good cook, too. He talked about the beans; she cooked them.

- **1 lb black beans**
- **2 sweet green peppers, cored, halved, white part removed; 2 halves left intact, the other 2 chopped**
- **1 medium-sized yellow onion, stuck with 2 cloves**
- **1 bay leaf**
- **¼ t oregano**
- **5 T olive oil**
- **1 medium-sized yellow onion, chopped**
- **1 clove garlic, minced**
- **salt to taste**
- **½ t sugar**
- **¼ c wine vinegar**

Pick over the beans and rinse three times. Soak in cold water 5 hours. Drain and place beans in a pot with the halved pepper, the onion stuck with cloves, bay leaf, oregano, and 2 tablespoons of olive oil. Barely cover the beans with cold water. Simmer on top of the stove, uncovered, for 1 hour or until beans are soft and there is very little liquid left in the pot. (While the beans are simmering, do not salt them. If the liquid cooks off, add a little more *hot* water. If cold water is added, the beans will harden.) In a saucepan heat remaining olive oil and sauté the chopped pepper, onions, and garlic, adding salt. When soft and golden brown, stir into the bean pot. Remove from the pot the pepper halves, the whole onion, and the bay leaf; discard. Stir in the sugar. Mash a few spoonfuls of the beans against the side of the pot and stir them into the beans so the sauce will be very thick. Stir in the wine vinegar; taste for seasoning, adding more salt if needed. Simmer, uncovered, stirring, for 15 minutes. Beans should not be soupy but should have a thick consistency. Serve with Pork Loin Cooked in Milk, Fried Plantains, and white rice.

BROCCOLI WITH ANCHOVIES

SICILY

Serves 6

1 large bunch broccoli
5 T olive oil
2 cloves garlic, chopped
4 anchovy fillets, drained, diced
¼ c dry white wine
salt and pepper to taste
4 T lemon juice

Separate the broccoli; peel stems with a vegetable peeler and wash them. Cut into pieces slightly larger than bite size. Cook in boiling, salted water 8 minutes. Drain well. In a saucepan heat the olive oil and sauté garlic and anchovies for 3 minutes. Add the cooked, drained broccoli and the wine. Season to taste with salt and pepper. Simmer, covered, until broccoli is tender. Stir in the lemon juice.

BRUSSELS SPROUTS WITH CHESTNUTS

ENGLAND

Serves 6

This dish, enjoyed with English farmers—the Brussels sprouts from their garden, the chestnuts from their trees—was served with a rib of roast beef from one of their steers, cooked in a simple, infallible way (see meat chapter).

1 qt Brussels sprouts
1 T salt
1 T chopped onion
½ t salt
2 c beef broth
4 T butter
⅔ c cooked chestnuts, cut in half

Soak the Brussels sprouts in 4 cups of cold water and 1 tablespoon of salt for 20 minutes. Drain and place them in a pot with the onions, the half teaspoon of salt, and the beef broth. Bring to a boil and cook, uncovered, for 5 minutes. Cover the pot, lower the heat, and simmer the sprouts for 10 minutes or until tender, checking several times so they do not get too soft. They should be tender but firm. Drain and keep warm. In a saucepan melt the butter, add the cooked chestnuts, and sauté until they are golden. Spoon the chestnuts and their butter sauce over the sprouts and mix well.

CARROTS AND ONIONS WITH CHICKEN BROTH

HUNGARY

Serves 6

Country people are cunning with seasonings. When they poach a large stewing chicken, the stock that they obtain is used in numerous ways. Here is a tasty dish, a way to spark up two vegetables—carrots and onions—with which few of us use much imagination.

4 c chicken broth
12 baby carrots, peeled
18 small white onions
1 small bay leaf
salt and pepper
2 T chopped parsley

Pour the chicken broth into a pot. Add the carrots, onions, and bay leaf. Cover the pot and simmer for 25 minutes over low heat or until the vegetables are tender. Season the vegetables to taste with salt and pepper. We have had them served plain out of the chicken broth, sprinkled with the parsley, and they are delicious. But a sauce can be made by blending butter and flour in a saucepan, then stirring in chicken broth, over low heat, until the sauce is smooth and thickened. Carrots and onions then are added to the sauce, simmered briefly, and then served in the sauce.

FRIED CAULIFLOWER

POLAND

Serves 6

1 2½- to 3-lb cauliflower, separated into flowerets
1½ t salt
¾ c milk
1 egg, beaten
⅔ c flour
fat or oil for deep frying

To a pot of boiling water, add salt and cook cauliflower for 10 minutes or until just tender but not too soft. Drain well. In a bowl blend milk, egg, and flour, stirring into a smooth batter. Dip the flowerets into the batter, shaking off the excess. Fry, completely submerged, in very hot deep fat for 5 minutes or until lightly browned. Drain on paper towels; serve immediately.

BRAISED CELERY, LEEKS, AND LETTUCE

FRANCE

Serves 6

6 medium-sized celery ribs, scraped
6 medium-sized leeks, white part only
salt and pepper to taste
2 T butter
1 c beef broth
3 small heads of Boston lettuce, cut in half

Arrange celery and leeks on the bottom of a pot in one layer. Sprinkle with salt and pepper. Dot with the butter. Pour in the beef broth. Cover the pot and simmer on top of the stove on low heat for 20 minutes or until the celery and leeks are slightly undercooked. Place lettuce between the celery and leeks, baste with the liquid, cover, and simmer for 10 minutes more (basting occasionally) or until the vegetables are tender. Taste for seasoning.

CHEDDAR POTATOES

ENGLAND

Serves 6

6 medium-sized potatoes, cooked, cut in medium-thick slices
3 medium-sized yellow onions, thinly sliced
salt and pepper to taste
1½ c grated sharp Cheddar cheese
1 t paprika
½ c melted butter

Place a layer of the potatoes on the bottom of a buttered baking dish, then a layer of onions. Season with salt and pepper; sprinkle on cheese. Continue with the layers, leaving ½ cup of the cheese for the top layer. Sprinkle on the paprika; pour the melted butter over all. Bake, uncovered, in a preheated 400-degree oven for 30 minutes or until the top is crisp and brown.

CHICK-PEAS AND HONEY

SYRIA

Serves 6

2 c chick-peas, soaked 5 hours, drained
2 T butter
1 T olive oil
1½ t salt
½ t pepper
¼ t cinnamon
½ c honey

In a pot simmer chick-peas, covered with water, 2 hours. Drain the chick-peas, place in a casserole, and blend thoroughly with the butter, olive oil, salt, pepper, cinnamon, and honey. Cook, uncovered, in a preheated 350-degree oven for 35 minutes.

DANISH POTATOES

Serves 6

Here's a quick one with a taste difference.

12 small new potatoes, boiled in their skins
2 T sugar
4 T butter
1 T warm water
2 T minced parsley

Drain and dry boiled potatoes; peel. In a saucepan, over medium heat, lightly brown sugar, stir in the butter and warm water, and blend well. Add the potatoes, turning them constantly until they are evenly coated and browned. Sprinkle them with the parsley.

STUFFED GRAPE LEAVES

GREECE

Serves 6

The peasants of the Middle East not only eat the grapes that they grow, but also they eat the leaves from the vines, stuffing them and cooking them in innumerable interesting ways, each country with its own techniques. The tasty results are called *dolmas* or *dolmadakias,* which is also the name they use for various stuffed vegetables. The grape leaves for this recipe can be found in many markets in jars.

1 lb lean lamb, ground twice
4 white onions, chopped
1 c uncooked rice
1½ t salt
½ t pepper
4 fresh mint leaves, chopped, or ½ t dry
1 c white wine
1 (1-lb) jar grape leaves
1 c beef broth
1½ T butter

In a bowl blend lamb, onions, rice, salt, pepper, and mint. Pour in the wine and mix thoroughly. Remove leaves from jar, drain, and wash well in cold water. Place a tablespoon of meat mixture in the middle of each spread leaf and roll tightly into a cylinder. In a casserole arrange the stuffed leaves in one layer if possible, in two if necessary. Pour in the beef broth and dot each leaf roll with butter. Place a heavy plate on top of the rolls to keep them from expanding too much as the rice cooks. Cover casserole tightly and cook in a preheated 300-degree oven for 1 hour. *Avgolemono* sauce is usually served with these *dolmas.*

Avgolemono Sauce

3 eggs
juice of 1 lemon
½ c stock from dolma casserole

In a bowl beat eggs and lemon juice together. When ready to serve the stuffed grape leaves, take the ½ cup of stock from the casserole in which they cooked and stir it into the beaten egg and lemon; place in a saucepan, barely simmer, stirring, until thickened; then pour over the stuffed grape leaves. Serve immediately.

HUNGARIAN GREEN BEANS

Serves 6

3 T butter
1 T olive oil
4 white onions, peeled, chopped
1¼ t paprika
3½ c tender young green string beans, cut into 1-inch pieces
1½ t salt
½ t pepper
1 c water
3 T flour
1 c sour cream

In a deep saucepan heat butter and oil and sauté onions until soft. Add paprika, string beans, salt, pepper, and water. Bring to a boil, cover the pan, and simmer 25 minutes or until the beans are tender. If there is any liquid left with the beans, pour it off. In a bowl combine the flour and sour cream, blending well. Stir the sour cream into the beans; barely simmer 5 minutes to heat. Do not boil.

LEEKS AND RICE

RUMANIA

Serves 6

2 T butter
1 T olive oil
2 small white onions, chopped
6 large leeks, white part only, cut in ¼-inch-thick slices
½ c uncooked rice
1½ c beef broth
1 t salt
½ t pepper

In a casserole heat the butter and oil and sauté the onions and leeks until golden. Stir in the rice and sauté 6 minutes. Pour in the beef broth and stir in the salt and pepper. Cover casserole and cook in a preheated 350-degree oven for 20 minutes.

MARIA CIFELLI LIMONCELLI'S PEAS WITH EGG AND CHEESE

Serves 6

1 (17-oz) can tiny peas, or 2 c (after being shelled) of fresh peas cooked in salted water until tender (reserve liquid)
1 T butter
1½ t salt
½ t pepper
1 t flour
2 small eggs
¼ c grated Parmesan cheese

In a saucepan heat the peas with 4 tablespoons of their liquid. Stir in the butter, salt, pepper, and flour. Simmer, stirring until the liquid thickens. In a bowl beat the eggs and the cheese together. Stir the egg and cheese mixture into the peas, simmering and stirring until the egg sets. Serve immediately.

PEPPERS WITH CHEESE

YUGOSLAVIA

Serves 6

1 lb sharp cheese, preferably goat's cheese
2 eggs, beaten
6 large sweet red peppers, cored, seeded, white parts removed
½ c cottage cheese
¼ c sour cream
½ t salt
1½ T olive oil

In a bowl break up the sharp cheese, crumbling it. Stir in the eggs, blending well. Stuff the peppers with the cheese-egg mixture. Mix together the cottage cheese, sour cream, and salt. Oil a casserole; arrange the peppers upright. Cover with the cottage cheese-sour cream mixture. Bake, covered, in a preheated 400-degree oven for 10 minutes; uncovered, bake for 10 minutes or until peppers are tender.

PISTO

SPAIN

Serves 6

1 c lean ham, diced
¼ c olive oil
3 medium-sized onions, sliced thinly
1 sweet green pepper, seeded, white part removed, diced
1 small eggplant, unpeeled, diced
2 small zucchini, unpeeled, diced
½ lb small green string beans
1 (1-lb) can tomatoes
salt and pepper to taste
2 T butter
3 eggs, beaten

Brown the ham in the olive oil; add the onion and pepper and cook until soft. Stir in the eggplant, zucchini, and string beans; cook 7 minutes. With your hands break up the tomatoes in a bowl; add to the other vegetables and ham. Season to taste with salt and pepper. Cover the pan and simmer 10 minutes; uncover and then simmer 15 minutes or until the vegetables are tender. In a frying pan melt the butter, add the beaten eggs, cook 3 minutes, turn them over, and cook until set. Serve this Spanish vegetable hash in warm plates with the eggs cut in thin strips and arranged on top of the vegetables.

FRIED PLANTAINS
(Green Cooking Bananas)
CUBA

Serves 6

3 (6-inch long) plantains, peeled
1½ t salt
lard for deep frying

Cut plantains in 1-inch-long pieces. Soak in salted cold water 15 minutes. Drain well and dry. In a deep saucepan melt lard and when very hot, fry (as you would French fried potatoes) until plantains are golden. Remove from fat and drain well on paper towels. When cooled somewhat, flatten out each piece with your fist (as if you were pounding a table, but not too hard), one restrained blow for each piece of plantain. Serve with Pork Loin Cooked in Milk and Black Beans and white rice.

PASQUALE LIMONCELLI'S POTATO SALAD

Serves 6

6 medium-sized potatoes, boiled in skins, cooled long enough to handle
¼ c olive oil
3 T dry white wine
1½ t salt
½ t pepper
4 T chopped parsley

Peel the potatoes while still warm (it improves the flavor when mixed with the dressing). Cut in ¼-inch slices and place in a bowl. In another bowl combine oil, wine, salt, pepper, and parsley. Blend well. Pour over the sliced potatoes.

MASHED POTATOES WITH ONIONS

POLAND

Serves 6

7 medium-sized potatoes, peeled, quartered
6 T butter
1 large yellow onion, peeled, minced
salt and pepper to taste

Cook potatoes in boiling salted water until tender. Pour off the water, dry thoroughly over medium heat, and mash. In a frying pan melt 3 tablespoons of butter and sauté the onions until soft. Add the onions in their butter and the remaining butter to the mashed potatoes. Season to taste and mix well.

HOT POTATO SALAD

FRANCE

Serves 6

8 medium-sized potatoes (new potatoes if possible), boiled in their skins

Dressing

(Mix while potatoes are boiling)
⅓ c olive oil
2 T wine vinegar
1 t salt
½ t pepper
1 garlic clove, peeled, crushed
1½ t Dijon mustard
½ t light brown sugar

In a bowl blend all dressing ingredients thoroughly. When potatoes are cooked and dried of all moisture over medium heat, peel them while they are still hot. This can be done by holding a potato on a fork with one hand and peeling the skin off with a sharp knife with the other hand. Dice the potatoes, as you prefer them, and toss well with the dressing. Remove garlic. Serve immediately while potatoes are still warm. Note: Dressing must be at room temperature. Do not refrigerate.

MASHED POTATOES AND SAUERKRAUT

HOLLAND

Serves 6

At first glance this may seem a prosaic pairing, but, truly, the proof is in the tasting.

6 medium-sized potatoes, peeled, halved
1½ t salt
3 T butter
½ c heavy cream
2 T butter
1 white onion, minced
1 (1-lb) can sauerkraut, well drained
1 c water

In a pot boil potatoes in salted water until tender. Drain well, replace on heat, and dry them thoroughly. Put dried potatoes through a ricer, place in a bowl, stir in butter and cream, and beat until creamy. In a saucepan melt butter and sauté onion until soft. Stir in sauerkraut and water, blending well. Cover pan and simmer for 35 minutes, stirring occasionally so sauerkraut doesn't burn and adding more water if necessary. When water has cooked off the sauerkraut and sauerkraut is tender, blend it well with the mashed potatoes and serve the combination very hot.

RATATOUILLE

FRANCE

Serves 8

This is a dish that is cooked according to where you are in France, but all the versions always include vegetables in season and always are dominated by eggplant. Said to be French, it is sometimes called *Ratatouille Niçoise* and is believed to have originated near Nice. As many of the cooks in that region are Italian, and as the dish is heavy with oil and garlic (and flavor!), we suspect that an Italian had a hand in it somewhere along the line.

1 c olive oil
6 small white onions, sliced thinly
4 medium-sized eggplants, cut in ¼-inch slices, then cubed
3 small sweet red peppers, cored, seeded, white part removed, cut in thin strips
1 small sweet green pepper, cored, seeded, white part removed, cut in thin strips
4 medium-sized zucchini, cut into ¼-inch slices, then cubed
3 cloves garlic, peeled, chopped
5 medium-sized very ripe tomatoes, peeled, seeded, chopped
salt and pepper to taste
½ t coriander seeds, crushed
4 fresh basil leaves, chopped
2 T fresh, chopped parsley

In a large saucepan heat the oil and sauté the onions until soft. Stir in the eggplant, peppers, zucchini, and garlic; cover pan and simmer for 35 minutes. Add the tomatoes and stir well, tasting for seasoning. This should be highly seasoned, but add the salt and pepper according to your own preferences. Stir in the crushed coriander seeds, cover, and simmer for another 25 minutes. Vegetables should be soft but not mushy. Stir in the basil and parsley; cook 2 minutes. This is served hot as a vegetable but is also delicious *cold* as an hors d'oeuvre. In some farm homes it is wrapped in crepes and served hot as a first course.

PASQUALE LIMONCELLI'S SPINACH WITH ANCHOVIES

Serves 6

2 (10 oz each) packages fresh spinach
6 T butter
4 anchovy fillets, chopped
1 clove garlic, minced
salt and pepper to taste

In a 4-quart pot bring 3 quarts of water to a boil. Add the spinach. Bring the water to a full boil again. Remove pot from the stove immediately. Lift spinach from the pot with a fork. *This technique is important.* Prepared this way, spinach will remain bright green and there will be little shrinkage.

In a saucepan melt butter and sauté anchovy fillets and garlic for 3 minutes. Stir in the spinach, season to taste with salt and pepper, blend well, and simmer for 5 minutes.

ZUCCHINI STUFFED WITH FETA CHEESE

BULGARIA

Serves 6

6 zucchini squash, 2 inches by 5 inches
2 T butter
½ lb feta cheese
1 large egg, beaten
1 T fresh, minced mint
½ t pepper
3 T bread crumbs
butter to dot top of stuffing
½ t paprika

Boil the zucchini in salted water for 15 minutes or until they can be easily pierced with the point of a small knife. Cool, slice in halves lengthwise, and scoop out a small amount of pulp from center the length of the squash. Chop the pulp and sauté in 2 tablespoons of butter until soft but not mushy. Cool the pulp. In a bowl mash the feta cheese, breaking up the large lumps; mix in the squash pulp, beaten egg, mint, pepper, and bread crumbs. Taste for seasoning, adding salt if necessary. Fill the zucchini shells with this mixture and place in a greased shallow baking dish in one layer. Dot with butter and lightly sprinkle over the paprika. Bake in a preheated 450-degree oven 20 minutes or until golden.

STUFFED ZUCCHINI

LEBANON

Serves 6

6 zucchini squash, about 2½ inches by 6 inches
3 T olive oil
1 medium-sized onion, chopped
1 large clove garlic, minced
salt and pepper to taste
1 T minced, fresh parsley
1 t minced, fresh mint
¼ t cumin
½ c rice, cooked al dente, slightly chewy
¼ c bread crumbs
½ c grated Parmesan cheese
1 (1 lb 12 oz) can tomatoes
½ c beef broth

Cut zucchini in half lengthwise; scoop out pulp, leaving a shell about ½ inch thick. Chop half of the pulp and discard the remaining pulp. Heat oil in a frying pan; add onion, garlic, and cut-up pulp from the squash; season to taste with salt and pepper and sauté until the onion is soft. Remove from the heat and mix in the parsley, mint, cumin, rice, bread crumbs, cheese, and one of the tomatoes from the can, mashed. Place the squash halves in a casserole. Divide the squash mixture into 12 equal portions and mound it in the squash shells. Break up the remaining tomatoes and mix them and their liquid with the beef broth. Spoon this mixture over the squash. Cover tightly with foil and the casserole cover and bake in a preheated 375-degree oven for 15 minutes. Baste and return to the oven for 30 minutes or until the squash shells are tender.

CHAPTER TEN

Desserts

The *contadini*, the country people, come full circle with dessert—taking it from their land when they can, as they do so successfully the main meal. Thus, their last course is often fruit, combinations of fruits, or pastry built around a fruit. The Austrians and Germans are lavish with another farm product, cream—they serve a lot of whipped cream with their sweets. The Middle Eastern people like to drench pastries in honey; the Spanish and Italians like custards and sweet cakes with fruit in them.

On feast days and other special occasions there is often a heavy touch with desserts. Strudels are popular and so are tortes and cheesecakes. Right to the end "those people who eat well," as Churchill referred to them, live up to their reputations. But they also know that most people seem to remember what happened "last" first, so mainly they keep desserts simple but memorable.

APPLES STEWED IN WINE

AUSTRIA

Serves 6

½ c Moselle wine
½ c water
1½ T lemon juice
1 T grated lemon rind (no white part)
1 c sugar
1-inch piece of cinnamon stick
6 large apples, peeled, cored, cut into ¾-inch slices, sautéed in butter 2 minutes on each side
1 cup of heavy cream, whipped

In a saucepan place the wine, water, lemon juice, rind, sugar, and cinnamon stick. Boil, uncovered, 6 minutes. In a baking dish place apples; pour the wine sauce over them. Bake, uncovered, in a preheated 325-degree oven for 20 minutes, basting. Serve warm with a dollop of whipped cream on top.

APPLE CAKE

CZECHOSLOVAKIA

Serves 6

¼ lb butter
1 c softened brown sugar
2 eggs, beaten
½ t vanilla
2 c flour
1 t baking soda
½ t salt
2 T lemon juice
3 T orange juice
1 t grated orange rind (no white part)
½ c walnuts, chopped
1 c tart apple, peeled, cored, chopped

In a bowl cream butter and sugar; blend in eggs and vanilla. In another bowl sift together flour, baking soda, and salt and stir into the creamed butter. Stir in the lemon and orange juices. Mix well. Add the orange rind, walnuts, and apples, mixing thoroughly. Grease a suitable cake pan and pour in the mixture. Bake in a preheated 375-degree oven 50 minutes.

APPLE FRITTERS

GERMANY

Serves 6

Batter

1 egg yolk
½ t salt
½ c beer
2 T sugar
¾ c flour
1½ T butter, melted
1 egg white, stiffly beaten

In a bowl whip egg yolk with salt, beer, and sugar. Slowly add flour, beating until the mixture is as thick as medium cream. Blend in the melted butter; let set 25 minutes. Blend in the beaten egg white. Use immediately.

Fritters

6 large tart apples, peeled, cored, cut in 1¾-inch slices
Oil for deep frying (amount depends upon the utensil used)
½ c confectioners' sugar

Heat the fat to 370 degrees. Dip apple slices in batter, coating well. Shake off excess batter. Fry a few at a time, turning them over so they brown on both sides. Remove (with a slotted spoon) and drain well. Serve warm, sprinkled with sugar.

PALMINA THOMPSON'S SOUR CREAM COFFEE CAKE

Serves 6 to 8

Remembering that Catherine de Médicis of Italy brought the art of baking (along with the fork and much of the art of cooking per se) to France when she married the Duke of Orleans there in 1533, it is not surprising that talented Palmina of Italian descent created her own famous coffee cake. She makes the topping first.

Topping

¼ c white sugar
⅓ c brown sugar
1 t cinnamon
½ c chopped pecans
½ c chopped walnuts

In a bowl place all ingredients and blend thoroughly.

Coffee Cake

¼ lb butter, softened
1 c sugar
2 eggs
½ pt sour cream
1 t vanilla
2 c flour
1 t baking soda
1 t baking powder
½ t salt

In a bowl cream the butter and sugar. Add eggs, sour cream, and vanilla; mix well. Blend in the flour, baking soda, baking powder, and salt. Pour half of the mixture into a square 9-inch baking pan, lightly greased. Sprinkle half of the topping mixture over it. Pour on rest of batter and sprinkle with the remaining topping. Bake in a preheated 350-degree oven 50 minutes.

DATE PUDDING

IRAQ

Serves 6

3 eggs, beaten
1 c sugar
1 c sifted enriched flour
1 t baking powder
¼ t salt
1 c chopped dates
⅓ c chopped walnuts
1½ T butter
1 c heavy cream, whipped

In a bowl beat the eggs and sugar until light. Stir in the sifted flour, baking powder, salt, dates, and nuts. Blend well. Grease an 8 x 8 x 2-inch baking pan with the butter. Pour the date mixture into it. Place in another pan with 1 inch of hot water. Bake in a preheated 350-degree oven for 50 minutes. Serve warm with whipped cream on top.

MACÉDOINE OF FRESH FRUIT

FRANCE

Serves 6

Often for dessert country folk simply set a bowl of fruit and cheese before guests. But sometimes when strawberries and raspberries are in season, rather than just drenching them in fresh clotted cream, they get a little fancy and prepare a *macédoine*. Frozen berries can be used but do not compare with the fresh ones.

2 medium-sized seedless, sweet oranges
1 pt fresh strawberries, hulled, washed, drained
1 pt fresh raspberries, washed, drained
½ c superfine sugar
¼ c brandy
⅓ c currant jelly
8 almonds, slivered, toasted

Grate a teaspoon of rind from an orange (not the white, just the outer orange peel). Peel the oranges, and divide into sections. In a bowl place grated orange, orange sections, strawberries, raspberries, sugar, and brandy. Blend well. Set the cup of currant jelly in a pan of simmering water, stirring until it dissolves. Arrange the mixed fruit in a serving bowl; pour the dissolved currant jelly over it, and chill in the refrigerator two hours. Garnish with the almonds before serving.

RIPE MELON WITH PORT

PORTUGAL

We like this with honeydew melon. But use the melon of your choice. A small cantaloupe would probably serve two. Work it out for yourself, figuring a half melon for each guest.

1 very ripe melon
2 t sugar
3 oz port wine
1 oz brandy

Slice the top quarter from the melon. Save it. Scoop the seeds from the melon. Discard them. Scoop out the melon meat and place in a bowl. Add the sugar, wine, and brandy. Toss well so the melon meat is marinated. Return the flavored melon meat to the shell. Replace the top as tightly as possible. Refrigerate for 3 hours.

BAKED FRESH PEACHES

ITALY

Serves 6

7 large, ripe peaches
5 T sugar
4 T butter
4 amaretti (Italian almond cookies), crushed
1 egg yolk, beaten
2 oz amaretto (Italian almond liqueur)

The extra peach is for the stuffing. Cut it in half and remove the pit and all of the pulp. Save the pulp. Cut in half and remove pits and one tablespoon of pulp from each of the other 6 peaches. Place that pulp (and all the pulp from the extra peach) in a bowl, sprinkle with the sugar, and mash well. Blend in the 2 tablespoons of butter, crushed *amaretti,* beaten egg yolk, and *amaretto.* Fill the peach halves with this well-blended mixture. Butter a baking dish with the remaining butter. Arrange the peaches in it and bake, uncovered, in a preheated 350-degree oven for 30 minutes. We like this dish hot, but it is equally good cold.

STEWED PEARS WITH HONEY AND ALMONDS

LEBANON

Serves 6

3 c water
1 c honey
juice of half a lemon
rind of half a lemon (not white part)
6 large, firm pears, pared, cored, and cut in half
½ c slivered almonds, toasted

In a saucepan place water, honey, lemon juice, and rind. Bring to a boil; boil 3 minutes. Reduce to a simmer. Place the pears in the saucepan and poach for 5 minutes. Remove from the heat; let the pears cool in the syrup in which they cooked. Serve cool with the honey syrup spooned over them and the almonds sprinkled on top.

TWO-LAYER PRUNE CAKE

POLAND

Serves 8 to 10

2¾ c sifted cake flour
1⅓ t baking soda
2 c sugar
1⅓ t cinnamon
1 t nutmeg
4 eggs
1⅓ c vegetable oil
1⅓ c buttermilk
⅔ t salt
2 c chopped cooked prunes

In a bowl sift flour, soda, sugar, and spices together. Beat the eggs for 1 minute. Add them and all other ingredients to the bowl with the flour. Beat 3 minutes. Pour into two lightly greased and floured 9-inch baking pans. Place in a preheated 350-degree oven for 45 minutes or until toothpick comes out clean. When cake is cool, sprinkle powdered sugar evenly over the top.

RUM MOLD

AUSTRIA

Serves 6

1-qt mold (placed in freezer 1 hour)
16 macaroons, crushed (stale, hard macaroons are best)
3 T white rum
3 c heavy cream, whipped
2 egg yolks, beaten
3 T confectioners' sugar

In a bowl place crushed macaroons, sprinkle with rum, and toss with two spoons until crumbs are well mixed with the rum. In another bowl place whipped cream and fold in the egg yolks and the sugar; then fold into the bowl with the macaroons, blending well. Remove mold from freezer, rinse, and shake out excess water. Spoon the whipped cream mixture into mold. Cover with wax paper and place in freezer 5 hours.

STRAWBERRIES IN CHIANTI WINE

ITALY

Serves 6

This is simple but superb. Strawberries must be fresh and very ripe. The Italian country folk use wild berries; the flavor inspires poetry.

2 pt strawberries, hulled, washed, drained
4 T sugar
1 c Chianti, chilled

In a bowl place strawberries, sprinkle them with sugar, and refrigerate for 3 hours. Fifteen minutes before serving add the wine. Blend. This sometimes is varied by slicing the strawberries and using ½ cup Marsala instead of the Chianti.

ZABAGLIONE

Serves 6

This was created in Italy, but several European countries have their own versions using different kinds of wine. It is served warm, and *immediately,* before it collapses. Serve in your best sherbet or wine glasses. There is a trick in timing to get it just right, but many master it in a couple of tries. It is also used in the country of its origin to spoon over hot puddings and cakes.

6 egg yolks
6 T sugar
1 T warm water
⅔ c Marsala wine

In the top of a double boiler place the eggs, sugar, and water over low, simmering water and very low heat. The bottom of the container with the egg mixture should not touch the water. With a wire whisk beat the eggs, sugar, and water until fluffy and pale lemon in color. Slowly pour in the Marsala, beating with the whisk constantly until the mixture forms in soft, creamy mounds. Spoon it instantly into the glasses, which should be waiting at your elbow. Rush to the table.

Index

C

D

E

J

K

L

M

T

V

W

Y

Z